Researching One's Chinese Roots in Hawaii

Proceedings of the 1985 Genealogy Conference in Hawaii

Edited by Kum Pui Lai and Violet Lau Lai

Hawaii Chinese History Center
Honolulu, Hawaii
©1988

Researching One's Chinese Roots in Hawaii
by the Hawaii Chinese History Center

ISBN-13: 978-1-953208-98-9

Hawaii Chinese History Center
111 N. King Street, Suite 307
Honolulu, HI 96817
808-521-5948

Reprinted in 2023 by:
ROLLSTON PRESS
1717 Ala Wai Blvd #1703
Honolulu, HI 96815
USA
www.rollstonpress.com

PREFACE ON REPRINT

2020 marked the semicentennial founding of the Hawaii Chinese History Center (HCHC). Unfortunately, this occurred in the midst of the COVID-19 pandemic and prevented any form of a celebration. Last year, in lieu of festivities, HCHC decided to reprint several rare, out-of-print books published decades ago. Due to the heavy demand, the very first is *Researching One's Chinese Roots, Proceedings of the 1985 Genealogy Conference in Hawaii*, which sold out twenty-five years ago.

This compilation served as a precursor to our Chinese Bicentennial Conference held at the University of Hawaii East West Center in 1988. It represents one of best resources in researching Chinese surnames, family genealogy, organizations and is the richest historical recollection of early Chinese families in Honolulu Chinatown, Kaneohe, Kahaluu, Punaluʻu, Waipahu, Waialua, Haleiwa, Kauai, Central Maui and Hilo. The conference lectures reflected the knowledge and experiences of many older Chinese who lived through the previous century. Nearly all have since passed away except for three individuals.

Hawaii Chinese History Center, the second oldest Chinese historical organization in America, was founded in 1970 by several Chinese professionals who wisely decided to record and preserve our unique Chinese history and heritage in the Hawaiian Islands. Their efforts resulted in a humble non-profit historical research center in Honolulu's Chinatown, which would thrive to serve the future generations.

HCHC's established goals were: 1) to stimulate interest and research among the Chinese in their own history, their experiences, and family genealogies in Hawaii, 2) to assist and guide Island Chinese to make their experiences available to the larger community through research, writing and publishing, and 3) to collect, inventory, record, and preserve historical materials, documents, and photographs of Hawaii's Chinese.

Over a half century later we reflect on our accomplishments: many publications, photographic exhibits, documentaries, cultural exhibits, endless history lectures, family history sessions, historic exhibitions, genealogy classes, research projects, conferences and most importantly serving the community and thousands of enthusiastic researchers who have sought our assistance.

I have been with the HCHC since its inception and served as president in the mid-1980s and continued to serve the center with hundreds of projects throughout the decades. Later, I returned to operate the center full time in 2010 after my retirement. Today I am the only survivor of the founding generation but continue to diligently maintain our thriving research organization.

With gratitude we thank our many patrons, donors, and loyal friends for their generosity in keeping our center solvent. Most importantly, we owe a great debt to our dedicated volunteers who have kept our center operating and have been most generous with their time and talents.

My most humble appreciation goes out to Randall K.H. Chun, a loyal volunteer, who has seen this project to its completion with his technical skills and immense hours perfecting the layout. Mahalo also to Gary R. Coover, author of *Honolulu Chinatown: 200 Years of Red Lanterns & Red Lights*, who assisted with the publication of this book.

With this reprint we honor our predecessors who founded our center, guided, and nurtured it to make it what it is today, and who have provided future generations a lasting legacy of our Chinese experience.

Douglas D.L. Chong

PRESIDENT OF THE HAWAII CHINESE HISTORY CENTER • FEBRUARY 2023

FOREWORD

THE CHINESE IN HAWAII constitute the first wave of immigrants from Asia to settle here. Much has been written about their coming as plantation laborers in the early 1850s, but little else has been written about the earlier arrivals of Chinese--as early as 1788 and 1789.

On December 6, 1788, the trading ship, the Iphigenia, and the schooner, North West America, entered at West Hawaii (Big Island) on their way home to South China from the Pacific Northwest.

Aboard the Iphigenia was Kaiana, a chief from Kauai, who had gone to China in 1787 and was now returning home. When King Kamehameha I realized that the schooner, North West America, was built on the shores of the Pacific Northwest by the Chinese crewmen, the Great King implored the captain to let these same crewmen build him a ship or two. What transpired between the King and natives, and officers and crewmen of the ships is not well documented from publications available to historians in Hawaii, but the ships' logs show very clearly that both ships departed Hawaii March 15, 1789.

In the three months that both ships were in Hawaiian waters, from December 6, 1788 through March 15, 1789, there is no reasonable doubt among historians that all healthy crewmen, including Chinese, would have come ashore to the aina of Hawaii. How many stayed to live in Hawaii and how many returned to the ships is not known, but it is this event that started the coming of the first Chinese to Hawaii.

And so it is in 1989 that the state of Hawaii will celebrate the bicentennial, or 200th anniversary, of the Chinese in Hawaii. The Hawaii Chinese History Center initiated the celebration of this momentous occasion through its planning committee of "Researching One's Chinese Roots": Larry F. C. Ching, Clarence F. T. Ching, Hung Dau Ching, Thomas Y. T. Chung, Helen Ing, Irene Johnson, Puanani Kini, chairperson, Violet L. Lai, Kam Man Leong, Albert N. Like, and Marie D. Strazar. Our warm mahalo to them and to the Board of Directors of the History Center for bringing this Conference to fruition.

The Hawaii Chinese History Center is privileged to be able to serve the community through the delivery of educational programs and publications on the Chinese in Hawaii, through its cadre of committed and professional volunteers. Among our valued volunteers are the librarian/researcher team of Kum Pui and Violet Lai, to whom we are deeply grateful not only for their regular dedicated work at the History Center, but also for their excellent work as co-editors of this publication.

Puanani Kini Woo
Executive Director

PREFACE

RESEARCHING ONE'S CHINESE ROOTS involves much work, time, and patience. Talking stories with grandparents, older relatives, and friends adds new dimensions to one's search. Repeated visits to the archives, Bureau of Conveyances, Department of Health, libraries, and courts provide basic documented information.

The July 27, 1985 Genealogy Conference spearheaded by the Hawaii Chinese History Center held at McKinley High School demonstrated that many people of all ethnic and racial backgrounds were keenly interested in the subject. There were 338 registered delegates with an attendance of close to 400 people.

These proceedings contain most of the papers presented at this first of a series of conferences and exhibitions leading to the grand bicentennial celebration in 1989 of the first arrival of the Chinese in Hawaii.

These presentations represent two important techniques in recording family history--first, the researched papers, and second, the personalized experiences of, "I remember when..." For both we are grateful, and we wish to thank all participants, especially the presentors, for adding to the history of Hawaii's Chinese.

The majority of the presentors provided personalized experiences as they recorded details of large and small Chinese communities, some no longer in existence, as the Chinese moved out to seek better economic opportunities. Most of their romanization of Chinese names and places follows local usage in Hawaii, generally of the Punti dialect. Differences in spelling reflect the variations used by persons and government agencies, and the new romanization used by the People's Republic of China.

May these records enable and inspire others to do likewise with their family history and consequently add to the missing pieces of the great mosaic which is the story of the Chinese of Hawaii.

Our thanks go to the presentors for sharing their experiences and research, to Puanani Kini Woo, mainstay and encourager, to Meg Wilkins for her editorial assistance and typing of the manuscript, and to all the others who made these proceedings possible.

The Editors
Kum Pui Lai
Violet Lau Lai

TABLE OF CONTENTS

CALLIGRAPHY by Marilyn Young Ching

CALLIGRAPHY ON COVER by Larry Ing

COVER DESIGN AND PHOTOGRAPHY by Lori L. Lai Ung Lai

GREETINGS

by THE HONORABLE JOHN D. WAIHEE

Lieutenant Governor, State of Hawaii *

John D. Waihee

THANK YOU FOR INVITING ME to speak at the Genealogy Conference sponsored by the Hawaii Chinese History Center. I know that all of you attending will be greatly helped by the information you receive here today on how to trace your ethnic roots.

In recent years, we have seen a reawakened pride in one's origins, a trend that has helped us keep alive the history and traditions of the immigrants who have contributed so much to our cultural diversity.

Genealogy studies of those immigrants, especially those who came from China, are so appropriate at this time. In 1989, we will be celebrating the 200th anniversary of the arrival in Hawaii of the first Chinese settlers, and any efforts that help us understand the contributions that they made to the shaping of modern Hawaii is invaluable.

There is another important reason for encouraging the study of our historical ties with China: as advances in communications and technology shrink our modern world, nations like China which seemed so far away yesterday are now our neighbors. And I can think of no better way to establish closer ties with an Asian neighbor like the People's Republic of China than to exploit the heritage we hold in common.

* The Hon. John D. Waihee was elected Governor of Hawaii in November 1986, a year after this Conference.

That heritage is being documented by the work you are doing, for as you research your Chinese roots, you are strengthening personal ties with your country of origin. You are also learning some very valuable things about a nation with which the State of Hawaii is forming new associations.

In recent months, I have been involved in efforts to bring about a new sister-state relationship with Guangdong, the southern province from which the greatest number of our Chinese immigrants came.

Actually, efforts to establish such a pact had their beginnings in 1980 when Hawaii's House of Representatives introduced a resolution to establish such a sister-state relationship with Guangdong, but the project was not advanced at that time.

When I visited the province in 1984, however, I conferred with Yang Li, Guangdong's Vice-Governor, on a wide range of economic, cultural, and social subjects from which we felt we could form the basis of a sister-state relationship.

Among the issues we discussed that were later incorporated in a formal agreement between Hawaii and the Province of the P.R.C. were:

* The formulation of a special tourism management program for Guangdong's leading tourism personnel to be conducted at the University of Hawaii's School of Travel Industry Management;

* The formation of a special task force from Hawaii to investigate the economic potential of Hainan Island with special emphasis on tourism;

* The possible participation of the People's Republic of China in our 1989 celebration of 200 years of Chinese immigration to Hawaii.

When I returned to Hawaii, I began work on the formal agreement which would set up an official sister-state relationship. That document also provided for exchanges of mutual benefit in the fields of economics, trade, science and technology, culture, education, sports, public health, and agriculture.

I am very happy to say that our work on this agreement was successfully concluded on May 21 of this year [1985] when Hawaii's Governor George R. Ariyoshi and Governor Liang Lingguang of Guangdong province signed the official sister-state Articles of Friendship in ceremonies held in Guangzhou.

An immediate result of the signing was an exchange visit last week from an official eleven-person delegation from Guangdong that included Governor Liang Lingguang and Deputy Consul Gau You Nian. Also visiting Hawaii were Chinese ministers for economics and trade, science and technology, tourism, and agriculture who had an opportunity to view Hawaii's development in their professional fields.

Other exchanges are scheduled to follow this first official visit and we have high hopes that these meetings will not only benefit both our areas economically, but will promote a lasting friendship between the people of the United States and China.

We are also focusing on cementing ties with another Asian country with which many Islanders have ethnic and historical ties. I am sure many of you know from the many celebrations being held this year that 1985 is the 100th anniversary of the arrival of the first Japanese contract workers. Therefore, we were very happy to be able to establish recently a sister-state relationship with Okinawa, an area which also contributed many new citizens to Hawaii. Our pact with this island province also provides for cultural and economic exchanges to benefit both our areas.

Here in Hawaii over the years, we have celebrated a number of anniversaries marking arrivals of immigrants from such countries as Portugal, Puerto Rico, and Korea. These occasions, besides observing historical dates, also remind us that we, or our forebearers, were all immigrants to these Islands; this is true even of our native Hawaiian citizens whose ancient ancestors arrived in great ocean-going canoes from Polynesian Islands to the south.

It is out of the great diversity represented by our immigrants that we have built a society that grants to all of us opportunities for a good life. And, through the good will of all our nationalities, we have created a society in which personal worth is judged less by our ethnic origins than it is by the content of our hearts and minds.

Here, our diversity unites us, rather than drives us apart, as happens so often elsewhere. And, although we may have life styles rooted in our varied ethnic backgrounds, or eat, worship or even speak differently, our plurality has enriched life here in Hawaii, instead of fragmenting it.

So, as you research your Chinese heritage here today, I wish you pleasure in discovering the rich history of your people. But, by the same token, I hope you will be led to a new appreciation of the other cultures that enrich our island life, for it is in seeking an understanding of our neighbors that we can create a unique new Hawaiian heritage that will benefit not only our children, but all the people who follow them.

Thank you for inviting me to share your Genealogy Conference with you today. Mahalo and aloha.

SOURCES FROM CHINA

THE ORIGINS OF CHINESE FAMILY NAMES

Yip-wang Law

THE CHINESE STARTED a system of hereditary family names several thousand years before the Europeans did. The earliest family names in China are believed to have come from totems, just like other civilizations in the world. In time, family names were derived from many other sources.

To cut the story short, let us skip the totems and start from the latter part of the New Stone Age, about 5,000 to 7,000 years ago. At that time the Chinese were living in a matrilineal clan society in the Yellow River Valley, and family names were used by women, and children inherited their mother's family name. Men were married away and played no important part in the family. Such a family name was called a xing (姓) in Chinese. Later, about 4,500 years ago, when society gradually fell into classes, men gradually replaced women as the center of society. Upper-class families began to adopt an additional family name for the male members of their family and such a family name was called a shi (氏) in Chinese. All descendants then carried two family names: a xing from the mother and shi from the father.

Then about 3,000 years ago came the Zhou dynasty when emperors began to create many feudal states for men of nobility to rule. Now men had firmly established themselves in the class society while women gradually dropped out of the game of family names. Eventually <u>xing</u> was applied to the male founder of a clan, who was usually also the founder of a feudal state or the ruler of a township, while each of its branches adopted a different <u>shi</u>. Such a distinction between <u>xing</u> and <u>shi</u> went on until China was unified into one empire and feudal states were abolished in 220 B.C. Meanwhile, the nobility from the past were all banished into commoners. <u>Xing</u> and <u>shi</u> have become one and the same thing since then.

1.   Family Names from Names of Ancient States

The most common source of Chinese family names is place names and, in particular, state names. There were already many small states in China when emperors of the early Zhou dynasty began a system of enfeoffment (分封制), in which an emperor invested the nobility with hereditary titles, territories, and slaves so that they could set up feudal states. About 800 such states were thus created early in the Zhou dynasty. But these states were often at war with each other, resulting in the annexation of the weaker ones by stronger ones. By the Spring and Autumn Period, only 170 or so remained. Down to the latter part of the Warring States Period, only seven remained. Qin, the most powerful of them, finally succeeded in conquering the rest of the states and unified China into one empire in 220 B.C. Thus ended the system of enfeoffment and all feudal states.

It was usually only after a feudal state had fallen and the descendants of its nobility had been scattered over the land that they began to adopt as their family name, the name of their original state. List 1 is a very incomplete list of Chinese family names of such an origin. In this list, as in all other lists to follow, each entry will consist of the family name in Chinese, followed by a number indicating its position in the well-known list, <u>A Hundred Family Names</u>, and finally followed by different ways of spelling it out in English. The spellings will be given in three groups, separated by slashes. The first group will be Putonghua (Mandarin) given in the new pinyin system, and the traditional Wade-Giles system will be given only when it differs from the pinyin system. The second group will be Cantonese, sometimes spelled in more than one way. The third group will be spellings in the Hakka dialect (marked by an *), the Southern Fujian dialect which is also spoken in

Taiwan (marked by a +), the Sze Yap dialect (marked by a =), and other ways of spelling. Due to lack of space, there will be no room for the founder, the location, the beginning and end dates of each of the states.

2. Family Names from Names of Ancient Townships, Counties, etc.

Like an emperor conferring hereditary titles, territories and slaves to his feudal lords, the feudal lords in turn also conferred the same, on a lesser scale, to his vassals. The territories conferred by a feudal lord were usually a township, or a county, or even something smaller. In the examples given in List 2, Cui and Lu were townships of the State of Qi; Fan and Wen were those of Jin; Feng and Yang were those of Zheng; Ma that of Zhao; Nie and Qi those of Wei; Qu, Ye, and Zhong those of Chu. However, Gan, Liu, and Mao were townships conferred directly by some Zhou dynasty emperors to their relatives. Similarly conferred by an emperor was Pang, a county. Lu was a county of the State of Qi. Ouyang was a ting, a subdivision of a county of the State of Yue. Fu, however, was not a conferred feoff (or fief). It was a plain place name. The Fu's got their family name from Fu Yan, the place where Fu Xue (a prime minister of the Shang dynasty) made his home.

3. Family Names from Official Titles

The English family name King is said to have come from the role some people played in dramas in medieval England. The Chinese equivalence Wang, meaning a king, however, was derived from the real thing. One clan of the Wangs can be traced back to Prince Bigong Gao, the 15th son of Emperor Wen of Zhou (about 1144 B.C.) whose descendants became rulers of the State of Jin. After Jin split into three smaller states, they continued to rule one of them, namely the State of Wei, until its annexation by the powerful Qin in 225 B.C. Since then, their descendants were scattered over the land and were known to their contemporaries as the Wang family, meaning the royal family. Another clan of the Wangs can be traced back to Prince Jin whose criticism of his father, Emperor Ling of Zhou (about 570 B.C.), brought him the banishment to be a commoner. Their descendants were also known to their contemporaries as the Wang family. Here Wang is only one example of many family names with multiple origins. Note that the family name Yang occurs both in List 1 and in List 2.

Limited space does not allow us to go into details about the known multiple origins of any family name considered in this article.

The family name Li can be traced back to a man called Jiu You who was a li-quan (理官 , grand justice) under Emperor Yao. One of his descendants, Li Cheng, changed the written form of his family name into its modern form 李 , which means a plum and is also pronounced li.

Emperor Yao served as a situ (a high official position in charge of land and labor force) under Emperor Shun before he came to the throne. Thus some of his descendants were known as Situ. But some source says that this position was not created until the early Zhou dynasty, more than 1,000 years after Emperor Yao.

Please refer to List 3 for the three family names discussed above.

4. <u>Family Names from Given Names, from Positions in a Family Tree, etc.</u>

A <u>xing</u> from the ancient times can become a family name later. Here are two examples:

Jiang: Jiang was the name of a river. Yan Di got this as his <u>xing</u> after he was born nearby that river.

Yao: Yao was the name of a marketplace. It was the birthplace of Shun Di and subsequently his <u>xing</u>. (Please refer to List 4.)

[Note: Both Jiang and Yao were written with the <u>nu</u> 女 or woman radical, indicating the fact that they were relics of a matrilineal clan society.]

Some family names were derived from the given name of the grandfather in the family. Consider the following examples from List 4.

Diao: from Shu Diao, a senior official of the State of Qi.

Gao: from Prince Gao of the State of Qi.

Long: from Long Wei, a minister under Emperor Shun.

Yu: from You Yu, a senior official of the State of Qin.

Courtesy names, a form of alias, were also a popular source of family names during the Zhou dynasty. Consider these examples from List 4.

Dong: from Dong Fu, a grandson of Huang Di.

Fang: from Fang Shu, a senior official of the Zhou dynasty.

He (pronounced as in <u>her</u>): At first there was the family name Qing from Qing Fu, a descendant of the Duke Huan of Qi. Later it was changed into He when the father of Emperor An of the Han dynasty was given the posthumous name Qing, as it was customary to regard posthumous names of deceased emperors as taboo. Both Qing and He mean to celebrate or to congratulate.

Lin: from Lin Kai, the second son of Emperor Ping of Zhou (about 770 B.C.). Another source says that this family name was derived from an episode. Please turn to the latter part of this article for details.

Pan: from Pan Chong, a descendant of the royal family of the State of Chu.

Sun: from Wei Sun, a grandson of the eighth son of Emperor Wen of Zhou. There were two more clans of Suns: one from the State of Chu, and the other from the State of Qi.

Each of the following three family names was derived either from the given name or from the courtesy name of someone.

Lei: from Fang Lei, father-in-law of Huang Di.

Wu: from Wu Can, a senior official of the State of Chu. Another source says that there was already an official named Wu Xu in the time of Huang Di.

Zhuo: from Zhuo Hua, a senior official of the State of Chu.

Towards the end of the Zhou dynasty, first the emperors, then the kings and other members of nobility were given posthumous names after their death. This also gave rise to a number of family names, such as the following.

Dai: from Duke Dai of the State of Song. Dai was also the name of an ancient state.

Jian: from Earl Jian of Xu of the State of Jin.

Yan: Originally there was the family name Zhuang (莊), from King Zhuang of Chu (Zhuang being his posthumous name). In 75 A.D. when Emperor Ming of the Han dynasty was given the posthumous name Zhuang, the Zhuangs had to change their family surname. They picked Yan as their new name. The Chinese phrase zhuang-yan means solemn. Years later some of the Yans changed back to their original name. There is a Zhuang-Yan Clansmen's Association in Hong Kong today.

One's position in a family tree can also give rise to a family name, such as:

Ding: from Dinggong Ji of the State of Qi. Ding was the fourth heavenly stem in the traditional Chinese calendar which is still in use today.

Gu: from Gugong Danfu, a prominent ancestor of the founders of the Zhou dynasty. Gugong means our ancient ancestor, and Danfu was his given name.

The name of a prominent clan of a royal family was the origin of the following family name.

Zuo: There was a Prince Zuo and a Prince You in the State of Qi. Zuo means left and You means right. Another source says that there was already someone called Zuo Che long before that time and that he was a petty official in Huang Di's time.

All the family names mentioned above are in List 4.

5. Family Names from Localities of Residence and from the Trades

We have seen geographic names of places used as family names. But the localities of one's residence can also serve as a family name, such as:

Guan: A gate. They surely lived by a gate because they were gatekeepers. The first man known to have such a family name was Yin Xi, the gatekeeper.

Qiu: A tumulus. A group of Jiang Taigong's descendants made their homes nearby a tumulus and adopted it as their family name.

The following two were from the trades.

Tu: A butcher. The first man known to have such a family name was Tu Kwei, a senior official of the State of Jin.

Wu: A witch doctor. The first man known to have such a family name was Wu Pang, Huang Di's witch doctor. See List 5 for all four.

6. Family Names of Other Origins and of Unknown Origin

List 6 and List 7 contain family names with at least two more new

9

origins. One new origin is from corruption in pronunciation (and consequently in written form). This happened occasionally when a clan was resettled in a new place where the native dialect was different and influenced the speech of the settlers. Another new origin is the change of a family name through an imperial decree. For example, a certain Mr. Jian (柬) was in a military expedition into Korea during the Tang dynasty and distinguished himself in drilling the Chinese troups. The Tang Emperor decreed that Mr. Jian's family name would be changed into Lian, which means drilling, to honor him for his specialty. Note that the character Jian is part of the character Lian and the two characters rhyme with each other.

Since there are so many family names and many of them have an origin that goes back thousands of years into history, naturally not all of them can be traced to their origins.

The number 000 in List 7 indicates that those family names are not included in the list called Bai Jia Xing (A Hundred Family Names). Bai Jia Xing (BJX) was compiled by an anonymous scholar of the Sung dynasty (960-1279) and has been made well-known to every household in China since it was often used as an introductory vocabulary text for school children in the old days. Despite its title, BJX contains 507 family names (i.e., 446 monosyllabic ones plus 61 disyllabic ones), which probably amounts to less than 10% of all the family names in China. It is interesting to note that some respectable American scholars in the field of family name studies, such as E. C. Smith, have very amusing ideas about the authorship, the contents, and the use of the BJX.

7.   Episodes in Family Names

The study of family names can be very fascinating when one comes across episodes like those in the following.

Earlier we saw that the family name Lin was derived from the courtesy name of a man called Lin Kai. Another source says that Emperor Zhou, a notorious tyrant at the end of the Shang dynasty, killed his uncle Bi Gan in order to silence him from giving moral advice. Bi Gan's son Jian fled for his life in a forest. Thus came the family name Lin, which means a forest.

Earlier we also saw that the family name Li was derived from the

10

official title Li-guan, meaning a grand justice, and that it was Li Zheng who changed its original written form into its modern written form which means a plum. One source goes further to give the circumstance under which the change was made. It says that Li Zheng offended the tyrannic Emperor Zhou of the Shang dynasty, and his son Li Zhen had to go into hiding and was able to avoid starvation only because he acquired a goodly supply of plums to eat. Thus he made the change in the written form of his family name in honor of the plums. Li Er, the philosopher better known as Lao Tze, was said to be a descendant of Li Zhen, eleven generations away.

The following three family names are from List 8.

Che means a cart. At the time of Emperor Wu of the Han dynasty, the Emperor gave special permission for his elderly Prime Minister Tian Qianqiu to ride in a cart to go to work in the court. Tian was thus known to his contemporaries as the Che Prime Minister, meaning the prime minister with a cart. His descendants adopted Che as their family name as a matter of honor.

The He's were descendants of the King of Han who ruled one of the seven states remaining in the latter part of the Warring States Period. After the State of Han was annexed by Qin, the Han descendants were scattered between the Yangtze and the Hui Rivers and took up Han as their family name. Local dialects in the south brought a corruption in the pronunciation of their family name, changing Han into He. The change was, according to one source, actually the result of an episode, not a corruption. It says that the policemen of the Qin Emperor caught up with the Hans when the latter were boarding a boat to flee for their lives. When approached by the policemen and asked to identify themselves, they were so scared that all they could do was point a finger at the river, meaning that their family name was Han (note that the Chinese word for cold was also pronounced han) as was the river. "So your name is He (note that the Chinese word for a river was also pronounced he), isn't it?" This was said to be the beginning of the family name He.

The family name Zhang was said to have derived from Hui, who was a grandson of Huang Di. Hui had invented the bows for shooting after being inspired by the Arc Stars. He was thus made an official in charge of making bows and also in charge of worshipping the gods in the Arc Stars.

He was thus honored with the family name <u>Zhang</u>, meaning a long or stretched bow. The Arc Stars, later known as the Zhang Stars, was one of the 28 constellations in ancient Chinese astronomy, which consisted of seven stars lined up in the shape of a bow. Six of these stars are part of the constellation Hydra in modern astronomy.

Cheng Qiao, a twelfth century scholar whose works have been a major source of reference for this article, rejected the episodes about the family names Lin, Li, He, and Zhang, on the grounds that it was simply not the way people acquired their family names at that time of history. He only accepted the episode of the family name Che.

Approximate Dates of Legendary Emperors
and Ancient Dynasties in China

炎帝	Yán Dì End of 32nd century B.C.
黃帝	Huáng Dì 2550 B.C.
堯帝	Yáo Dì 2297 B.C.
舜帝	Shùn Dì 2179 B.C.
夏	Xìa 21st cent. to 16th cent. B.C.
商	Shāng 16th cent. to 1066 B.C.
周	Zhōu 1066 to 256 B.C.
西周	Western Zhōu 1066 to 771 B.C.
東周	Eastern Zhōu 770 to 256 B.C.
春秋	Spring & Autumn Period 722 to 481 B.C.
戰國	Warring States Period 403 to 221 B.C.
秦	Qín 221 to 206 B.C.
漢	Hān 206 B.C. to 220 A.D.

List 1. Family Names from Ancient State Names

蔡	155	Cài (Tsai)/ Choy, Choi/ Chai*, Choa[+]
曹	26	Cáo (Tsao)/ Tso, Cho/ Chao*, Tzo[+]
陳	10	Chén/ Chan, Chun/ Ching*, Chinn*, Dan[+], Tan[+]
成	115	Chéng/ Sing/ Sing[+]
程	193	Chéng/ Ching/ Tia[+]
鄧	180	Dèng (Teng)/ Dang/ Ten*, Tenn*, Ding[+], Ong*
杜	129	Dù (Tu)/ Do, Doe, Doo, To/ Tu*, Do[+]
郭	114	Guō (Kuo)/ Kwok, Kwock/ Gwock*, Gue[+]
韓	15	Hán/ Hon/ Hon*, Han[+]
洪	184	Hóng (Hung)/ Hung/ Fung*, Ang[+]
胡	158	Hú/ Wu, Woo/ Fu*, O[+], Hoo (Vietnamese: Ho)
黃	96	Huáng (Hwang)/ Wong/ Wong*, Eng[+]
黎	262	Lí/ Lai/ Lee*, Le[+] (Vietnamese: Le)
梁	128	Liáng/ Leong, Leung/ Leong*, Niu[+]
廖	342	Liào/ Liu, Lew/ Lyau*, Liau[+]
羅	75	Luó (Lo)/ Law, Lo, Loh, Low, Lowe, Lor/ Lo*, Lo[+]
莫	168	Mò/ Mok, Mock/ Bok[+]
歐	361	Ōu/ Au/ Aeou*, Aiu*, Au[+]
彭	47	Péng/ Pang/ Pang*, Pi[+]
容	336	Róng (Jung)/ Yung/ Young, Yung[+]
阮	130	Ruǎn (Juan)/ Yuen/ Ng[+] (Vietnamese: Nguyen)
宋	118	Sòng (Sung)/ Sung/ Soon*, Soong*, Sung[+]
譚	293	Tán/ Tam, Tamm, Tom, Thom/ Tam*[+], Harm*
吳	6	Wú/ Ng, Eng, Ing/ Ng*, Ngo[+]
蕭	99	Xiāo (Hsiao)/ Siu, Shiu, Seu, Sheu/ Seo*, Hsiao[+]
謝	34	Xiè (Hsieh)/ Tse, Jay/ Char*, Sia[+]
徐	150	Xú (Hsu)/ Tsui/ Chee*, Chi[+]
許	20	Xǔ (Hsu)/ Hui/ Hee*, Co[+], Ko[+]
薛	68	Xuē (Hsueh)/ Shit, Sit/ Si[+]
楊	16	Yáng/ Yeung, Young/ Yong*, Yeo[+], Yu[+]
趙	1	Zhào (Chao)/ Chiu, Cheu/ Chow*, Deou[+], Dio[+]
曾	385	Zēng (Tseng)/ Tsang/ Zane*, Zen*, Tzan[+]
鄭	7	Zhèng (Cheng)/ Chang, Cheng, Jang, Jeng/ Chang*, Tsang*, Di[+]
周	5	Zhōu (Chou)/ Chau, Chow, Jow/ Chu*, Jiu[+]
朱	17	Zhū (Chu)/ Chu/ Chu*, Ju[+], Gee*

List 2. Family Names from Names of Ancient Townships, Counties, or Ting

崔	189	Cuī (Tsui)/ Tsui, Chui/ Chui+ (Korean: Choi)
范	46	Fàn/ Fan/ Farm*, Huan+ (Vietnamese: Pham)
馮	9	Féng/ Fung/ Bang+
傅	84	Fù/ Fu, Foo/ Bo+
甘	245	Gān (Kan)/ Gum, Kum, Kam/ Gam+
劉	252	Liú/ Lau/ Liu*, Lau+
盧	167	Lú/ Lo, Low/ Loo*, Lo+
馬	52	Mǎ/ Ma, Mah, Mar, Marr/ Ma*+, Be+
毛	106	Máo/ Mo/ Mau*, Mo+
聶	372	Niè (Nieh)/ Nip/ Nap*
戚	33	Qī (Chi)/ Chik/ Chek+
屈	124	Qū (Chu)/ Wat, Watt, Wut/ Kut+
溫	321	Wēn/ Won, Wun/ Won*, Wun+
楊	16	Yáng/ Yeung, Young/ Yong*, Yeo+, Yu+
葉	257	Yè (Yeh)/ Yip, Ip/ Yap*+
鍾	149	Zhòng (Chung)/ Chung, Jung, Chong, Jong/ Chung*, Jung+
陸	198	Lù/ Look, Luk, Luke/ Look*, Liok+
龐	120	Páng/ Pong/ Bang+
歐陽	412	Ōuyáng/ Auyeung, Auyoung/ Auyung+

List 3. Family Names from Official Titles

王	8	Wáng/ Wong/ Wong*, Ong+
李	4	Lǐ/ Lee/ Lee*+, Li+ (Korean: Lee, Rhee)
司徒	439	Sītú (Szetu)/ Seto, Seeto, Szeto/ Sue-to*, Sih-do+
		(Not to be confused with the Japanese name Shito)

表四、 以姓、以名、以字、以謚、以次爲氏

List 4. Family Names from Xing, from Given Names, from Alias, from Posthumous Names, and from Positions in a Family Tree

姜	32	Jiāng (Kiang)/ Keung/ Keong*, Keung+
姚	101	Yáo/ Yiu/ You*, Yeo+
戴	116	Dài (Tai)/ Dai/ Dy*, Dye*, De+
刁	148	Diāo (Tiao)/ Diu, Dew/ Tyau* , Diao
董	127	Dǒng (Tung)/ Tung, Tune, Dong, Dung/ Dang+
方	56	Fāng/ Fong/ Hong*, Beng+
高	153	Gāo (Kao)/ Ko/ Gao*, Go+
賀	70	Hè (Ho)/ Ho, Hor/ Fo*, Ho+ (Pronounce He as in Her)
雷	69	Léi/ Lui, Loui, Louei/ Lui*, Lui+
林	147	Lín/ Lam, Lum/ Lim*+
龍	256	Lóng (Lung)/ Lung/ Liong+
潘	43	Pān/ Poon, Pun/ Pua+
孫	3	Sūn/ Suen, Sun/ Sun*, Suyn*, Soon+, Sun+
伍	89	Wǔ/ Ng, Eng, Ing/ Ng*, Ngo+
余	90	Yú/ Yu/ Yee*, Yi+
袁	59	Yuán/ Yuen, Yuin/ Yen*, Yuan+
簡	382	Jiǎn (Chian)/ Kan/ Gahn*, Kahn*, Gan+
嚴	27	Yán/ Yim/ Yan*, Giam+
丁	177	Dīng (Ting)/ Ting, Ding/ Dan*, Ding+
古	338	Gǔ (Ku)/ Goo/ Goo*, Go+
左	187	Zuǒ (Tsuo)/ Tso/ Tso+
卓	277	Zhuō (Chuo)/ Cheuk, Chock/ Chock*, Do+

表五、 以所居、以技爲氏

List 5. Family Names from Localities of Residence and from Trades

關	394	Guān (Kuan)/ Kuan, Kwan, Kwon, Quon/ Kwan*, Guan+
邱	151	Qīu (Chiu)/ Yau/ Heu*, Hiu*, Ku+
屠	297	Tú/ Tu, To, Toe/ Du+·
巫	220	Wū/ Mo/ Moo*, Bu+

表六、 未知由來的氏
List 6. Family Names of Other Origins and Unknown Origins

| 詹 | 254 | Zhàn (Tsan)/ Jim/ Jam*, Jiam+ (From the Mayor of Zhan, a township of Chu) |
| 佘 | 488 | Shé / Sah/ - (From unknown origin, or a corruption of the family name Yu 余) |

表七、 《百家姓》漏列的氏
List 7. Family Names not Listed in "A Hundred Family Names"

鄺	000	Kuàng/ Kong/ Kong*, Fong (An ancient state)
練	000	Liàn/ Len, Lin/ Len*, Lein+ (An ancient township; also from the family name Jian 柬)
倫	000	Lún/ Lun/ Loon*, Lun+ (From Ling Lun, a musician in the time of Huang Di)
麥	000	Mài/ Mak, Mark/ Be+ (Descendants of Mai Tezhang, a 6th century general)
區	000	Ōu/ Au/ Aeou*, Aiu*, Au+ (A corruption of the family name Qu 歐, after Ou Yezi)
檀	000	Tán/ Tan/ - (An ancient township)
冼	000	Xiǎn (Hsian)/ Sin, Sinn, Shin/ - (Unknown origin; or a corruption of the family name Xi 洗)
禤	000	Xuān (Hsuan)/ Huen/ - (Unknown origin)
招	000	Zhāo (Chao)/ Chiu, Jiu/ Jio+ (Descendants of Bu Zhao of the state of Jin)
植	000	Zhí (Chih)/ Chik/ - (Descendants of the King of Yue)

List 8. Family Names with an Episode   表八、 以事爲氏

車	229	Chē (Cheh)/ Che/ Chia+
何	21	Hé (Ho)/ Ho, Hor, Hoe/ Ho+ (Pronounce He as in Her)
張	24	Zhāng (Chang)/ Cheung, Cheong/ Chong*, Jong*; Dew+, Teoh+, Diu+, Chung+

LOCATING ONE'S ANCESTRAL VILLAGE

Douglas D. L. Chong

I. SEARCHING FOR THE ANCESTRAL VILLAGE

  A. Geographic Background

      Kwangtung, the homeland of 90% of local Chinese, is only one
      state in China; it contains 70 separate counties. Do not be
      fooled into thinking Kwangtung is your village, as so many third
      and fourth generation Chinese swear it is. It's like telling
      someone your village is Hawaii, rather than the more precise--
      Carlos Long Tract of Palolo Valley, of Kaimuki District, City of
      Honolulu, Hawaii. Worse yet is to say you are from Canton, the
      capital of Kwangtung province; the majority of our ancestors
      have never even visited Canton in their lifetime. One must be
      able to pinpoint the exact village, hamlet, then county. This
      is the primary focal point you must ascertain through research
      conducted with family history, ancestral clubs, family friends,
      surname associates, and family gravestones.

      [At this point, copies of ancient and rare Chung Shan maps, as
      well as the newest Spring 1985 map of Chung Shan just brought
      out of China, were distributed for the following portion of the
      lecture.]

  B. Sub-districts of Chung Shan

      A great number of both local "Hakka" and "Punti" types hail from
      Chung Shan, one of the 70 counties of Kwangtung located due west
      across the river from Hong Kong. The boundaries of the very old
      hamlet defined ten separate "doo" or sub-districts still very
      familiar to the Hawaii Chinese as Leong Doo, Yun Doo, Duck Doo,
      Gook Doo, Kung Sheong Doo, Larm Doo, Wong Leong Doo, Loong Doo,
      See Jee Doo and Dai Jee Doo which combined to form See Dai Doo.
      According to present day "kee" or divisions, the system and some
      of the demarcation lines have changed: Leong Doo combined with
      Yun Doo is termed "dai yut kee" or Kee No. 1; Loong Doo is Kee
      No. 2; Larm Doo is Kee No. 3; See Dai Doo is Kee No. 4; Gook Doo
      is Kee No. 5; Kung Sheong Doo is Kee No. 6; the southern
      outlying islands became Kee No. 7; Wong Leong Doo became Kee No.
      8; and the low-lying northern sandbar islands of North Chung
      Shan became Kee No. 9.

  C. Sub-linguistic/Ethnocultural Groups

      As we review the newest map of Chung Shan County defined by the
      People's Republic of China, we note the many types of boundary
      divisions and the name changes applied to many villages. There
      are many areas of Chung Shan occupied by various sub-linguistic/

ethnocultural groups, such as the Hakka, the Nam Long, the Sam Heong, the Loong Doo, and the Sam Chau groups.

Many other districts were homelands to first generation Chinese in Hawaii, such as--

Sam Yup, the area surrounding Canton City itself, is comprised of Nam Hoy, Pun Yu, and Sun Duck.

See Yup, the large district due west of Chung Shan County, is made up of Toi Shan with its ten large hamlets, Sun Wui with eight hamlets, Yun Ping, and Hoi Ping with four hamlets.

Hakka Districts are Pun Yu, Tseng Sing, Pok Lo, Wai Chau, Tung Kun, Pao On, Fah Yuan, Moi Yen, and many other districts.

II. RESEARCHING THE PAST

A. Check Relatives, Friends, and Associates

In searching for informants, first check the closest living, older relations in Hawaii. Then check other informants-- granduncles, aunts, their offspring, clan and kin associates, district or neighbor friends of the older generation, social group associates, business associates, dialect or geographic organizations. Record all details and leads either on tape or notes ideally to be recorded onto disks for the computer.

B. Check Tombstones

Graveyard inscriptions are a very valuable source, especially if the grave is old, or where the old practice deemed that many forms of the deceased's names, village, county, and pertinent dates all be inscribed on the monument. Another old practice was to inscribe the names of the sons, daughters, grandsons, and great-grandsons on the lower left-hand corner of the tombstone, which makes an excellent family tree. Take good pictures, rubbings, and notes so that the person helping you to translate the Chinese characters later can do an accurate job.

C. Check Written Records

Written records, for example, birth certificates which may even date back to the period of the Hawaiian Kingdom, and death certificates, are both available from the State Department of Health for a small fee. Search out old personal letters, land deeds, ancestral books, society and organization membership certificates. Also, all Chinese in an April 30, 1900 act were required to be photographed for a Certificate of Residence by the U.S. Internal Revenue on Form 478, and for another Certificate of Identity by the U.S. Department of Commerce and

Labor on January 14, 1908. I have found many Chinese families in possession of these. Also some families have produced original passports of labor, merchant certificates, and business permits.

There are thousands of immigration records at the State Archives. There are also passports with photographs, as well as exit permits, return permits, Hawaiian-born-Chinese records, permits for minors, contract labor permits for rice, taro, pineapple, and sugar laborers, women and picture bride permits, Board of Immigration passports issued in Hong Kong, residence bonds, permits to enter, and naturalization certificates. Passengers on ship manifests are indexed by names. There is a wealth of material here, with not only the forementioned records but also old documents, articles, and directories. For real estate and personal property, check the Bureau of Conveyances. Expect to put in months and even years doing basic research, and be patient!

Several branches of the Mormon Church in the Islands have excellent facilities and "tons" of records from all over the world on microfilm. Two of their most useful records are the U.S. Censuses of 1900 and 1910 which list Chinese by households, complete with birthdates and year of arrival, children, their names and ages, as well as years of schooling.

D. Names

A very important thing to know is that the old Chinese, especially the men, went by many types of names: milk name, given name, school name, marriage name, and various other cognomen. Be sure you get as many names as possible, since the majority of all records found do not list your ancestors by the names by which you know them. Also the English transcriptions of Chinese names often turn up with five different spellings, usually the result of misunderstood Chinese syllables.

III. MAKING A VISIT TO THE VILLAGE

A. Be sure you obtain several maps of the region; a broad map in English will help no one. Be certain of the village name, as it may have changed since the days your ancestors left. Locate it on the map, identify the county it is located in, the correct "kee" and marketplace. Have all of this transcribed into Chinese and into modern terminology, from village into co-op, from hamlet into commune, from "doo" into "kee," etc.

B. Define general localities. No one is going to do it for you. For instance, Nam Long is not enough; there are nearly 50 villages spread over many miles. Sam Jau, although an island, is not enough; there are over 20 villages and you won't have time to take a taxi to all the villages looking for your grandfather's house. With correctly written Chinese characters, you'll have little problem; strangers along the way are very helpful.

C. Ways to get to the village in Mainland China.

1. Obtaining an individual visa is difficult unless you are very fluent in both written and spoken Mandarin.

2. Obtaining an overseas Chinese visa or getting a visa as a U.S. citizen with American passport returning to China to visit relatives is not very difficult, but be sure you speak the local dialect well or go with someone who does. It is very inexpensive to get to the village this way, as you can bypass China Travel Service and the tour agencies. You can go by railway to villages north of Hong Kong or by hydrofoil to Chung Shan. The hydrofoil goes directly to Jee Hoy, Gau Jau and bypasses Macau. Do not go to Hong Kong by yourself or with a tour and expect to get a visa to China easily; it takes several days and much unnecessary expense. Apply to the Chinese Consul in San Francisco while you're in Hawaii; it is much cheaper and there is no wait or bother in Hong Kong or at the border.

3. Visa through group application. You are now at the mercy of your tour group and travel accommodations arranged by the Chinese. It may also cost more money for a guide and a driver. If you depart from the tour to go to the village, the ride will take hours on dirt roads and ferry crossings. However, if you don't speak Chinese or don't have a guide who does, you don't have much choice, except by this method.

D. What to Expect in China

1. Hotel accommodations are generally very good in Chung Shan. There are good hotels in Jee Hoy, Wun Chin in Sam Heong, Choy Hang Bun Goon in Choy Hang Village, and there are two large hotels in Shekki. Food, rooms, and shopping are good. Be sure to plot your route and trip ahead of time. The Chinese drivers are not at all accommodating; also, they are very indifferent and very skilled at the practice of "acting dumb." You will be able to see and do much more if you are in command. I usually get to visit with relatives in six to eight different villages in one day if I maximize the opportunity and minimize driver-rider interaction.

2. Villages usually have no ancestral records left; practically everything was destroyed during the Cultural Revolution. Gravesites have no original monuments, as they, too, were destroyed. There are some photos left as well as big, beautiful, old ancestral portraits, so be prepared with a copy lens for your camera.

3. The biggest attractions are your remaining relations who have detailed oral history memories. Write up your notes right there, and use a prepared list of questions you want answers to. Discuss your knowledge of your ancestors; they'll add valuable details of history sometimes going back five generations. Take time to draw out a rough family tree with them. This way you'll know where they are and they'll also be able to supply the names of ancestors long forgotten. Remember, these elders are a dying breed of oral historians, since the TV age has already hit the villages! The best experience is to stay in the village for a few days.

IV. SIGNIFICANCE OF THIS EXPERIENCE

1. Visiting the village will provide you and your family a meaning to the past.

2. It will foster a meaningful depth to your personal identity. After you have gone through all this research and visited the village back in China, you will gain a proper perspective in understanding your "Tai Po" and "Tai Goong" and their lifestyle, philosophy, and values.

3. It will create a stepping-stone to Chinese culture, ethnic pride, and heritage which broadens one's horizons within the family of man.

GENERAL SOURCES IN HAWAII

CHRONOLOGY OF SIGNIFICANT EVENTS OF THE CHINESE IN HAWAII

Tin-Yuke Char

1778   Captain James Cook discovered a flourishing culture in the Hawaiian Islands.

1788   The Felice, a British registry, arrived in Hawaii October 18 and departed October 26; John Meares, Master.

1788   The Iphigenia, a British registry, arrived in Hawaii December 6; William Douglas, Master.

The North West America, a British registry, arrived in Hawaii December 6 accompanying the Iphigenia; Robert Funter, Master.

1789   The Iphigenia and North West America departed from Hawaii March 15.

1802   A Chinese introduced a primitive sugar mill on the Island of Lanai.

1810-1825   Sandalwood was traded with China. Hawaii became known as Tan Heong Shan 檀香山 , "Sandalwood Mountain," to the Chinese.

1852   Captain Cass of the bark Thetis arrived from Amoy with the first contract laborers for the sugar plantations.

1856   Chinese merchants gave a grand ball in honor of King Kamehameha IV and his bride, Queen Emma. Chun Afong 陳啊芳 was one of the leaders.

1881   King Kalakaua visited China on his trip around the world. He was entertained by Viceroy Li Hung-Chang 李鴻章 in Tientsin.

1882   Sun Tai-cheong 孫帝象 (later known as Sun Yat-sen 孫逸仙) graduated from Iolani School.

1884   United Chinese Society 中華總会館 organized.   Leaders included Goo Kim 古今輝 and Ching Lee 程利

1894   Dr. Sun Yat-sen returned to Hawaii and organized the Hing Chung Hui 興中会 , a revolutionary society.

1900   Chinatown plague and fire.

       Liang Chi-chao 梁啟超 organized the Protect Emperor Society 保皇会 in opposition to Dr. Sun's revolutionary movement.

       A Chinese newspaper, Sun-chung-kwok-bo 新中国報 , was started by Liang Chi-chao.

1911   Chinese language schools, Mun Lun 明倫 and Wah Mun 華文 started.

1912   Dr. Sun Yat-sen chosen provisional President of the New Chinese Republic 中華民国 .

1929   First publication of The Chinese in Hawaii 檀山華橋 , bi-lingual: best source of biographical sketches of community leaders.

1939   Chinese community celebrated its 150th anniversary of Chinese arrivals.

1959   Hawaii Statehood.

       Hiram L. Fong 鄺友良 , first Chinese elected to U.S. Senate.

1961   50th anniversary of the Chinese Chamber of Commerce 檀山中華商会 Edited by Robert M. Lee 李文華 . 五十週年紀念刊

1970   Hawaii Chinese History Center founded.

1975   The Chinese of Hawaii: a checklist of Chinese materials in UH Library
                by Chau-Mun Lau 刘秋霎 .

1984   United Chinese Society Centennial Directory published. 中華總会館百週年特刊 Edited by Toy-Len Chang 鄭彩蓮

1985   Hawaii Chinese History Center sponsored Genealogy Conference.

GENEALOGICAL SOURCES AT THE HAWAII STATE ARCHIVES

Mary Ann Akao

GOOD MORNING! I'm happy to be here to share with you some of the documentary sources that Violet Lai, a previous speaker, used in the State Archives. I'll be showing slides of records that can be used for genealogical research.

The presentation will be in two sections. The first set of slides is taken from a slide-tape show called, "Tools to Compile Your Family Tree." It is an introduction to the kinds of records that may be used for genealogical research and to the information contained in each series of records.

The second set of slides is of various permits issued by the Foreign Office, more particularly the Chinese Bureau; these permits were cancelled upon entry of the bearer to Hawaii. These records are a product of laws restricting Chinese immigration to the Hawaiian Islands beginning in the 1880s. They need extensive work to make them usable, but are shown today to acquaint you with different possibilities available in documentary sources.

Before beginning, however, I'd like to say a few words about the nature of archives and procedures for use at the State Archives.

The term "archives" refers to the official record of an organization and is created in the course of doing business. It may be the archives of a business, e.g., People's Ice and Refrigerating Company; a religious denomination, e.g., the Episcopal Church; an organization, e.g., Hawaii Chinese History Center; or government, e.g., the Government of the Hawaiian Islands. These records document and illustrate the purposes for an organization and how those purposes were carried out. For example, if governments safeguard personal and property rights, records are kept on births and naturalization as proof of citizenship; wills and deeds are filed as a record of transfer of property. If a government regulates or controls an activity, such as the immigration of Chinese, careful records are kept of those who enter and leave the country.

Therefore, the State Archives, as a depository of government records, usually has information on people only when some aspect of their lives involves dealing with the state government or its predecessors, the Territory of Hawaii, The Republic of Hawaii, the Provisional Government, or the Kingdom of Hawaii.

Secondly, because archives document an activity, they are kept in the order they were used in the office that created them. They are not separated by subject. For this reason, you will not find all of the information on a particular person in one file. Archives (as an institution) keep a variety of indexes or other finding aids to give researchers access to the information contained in different series of records.

A third feature of archives that I'd like to stress is that archives are unique. Unless you are asked to use a microfilm copy, there is usually only one copy of the document. Especially before the advent of photocopying, they did not exist in multiple copies. For this reason, we have procedures that we ask patrons to follow to safeguard the records.

On your first visit to the State Archives, you will be asked to fill out a registration card. Before you enter the Index or Reading Room, you will be asked to check in briefcases and large containers. With the exception of library books and microfilms, all documents must be requested on call slips. Then, to prevent documents from being disordered, only one folder is issued at one time. Also you will be asked to use pencils only and to handle the documents very carefully. Copy service by the staff is available for a charge. You may search on your own, but if you need any help, an archivist is at the reference desk to answer questions or suggest additional sources of information.

With these introductory remarks, we can begin with "Tools to Compile Your Family Tree." These are available at the State Archives. You can follow the flow chart included in the packet of handouts.

Slide 1: This is the Hawaii State Archives. We are a division of the Department of Accounting and General Services. We are located on the Mauka-Diamond Head corner of the Iolani Palace grounds in the Kekauluohi Building. The Archives is open from 7:45 a.m. to 4:30 p.m. Monday through Friday.

Slide 2: The easiest place to begin is at the Vital Statistics Index. The cards are in catalog drawers with blue labels. There are separate indexes for births, deaths, and marriages that appeared in the newspapers. The cards within the drawers are arranged alphabetically by the first letter of the person's last name. Unfortunately, not many immigrant names were picked up.

Slide 3: This is an index card of a birth announcement. It gives information on the date of birth, place of birth, and names of parents.

Slide 4: This is an index card of a marriage announcement that appeared in the Honolulu Advertiser on January 21, 1934. It gives information on the date of marriage, place of marriage, and names of the male and female.

Slide 5: This is an index card of a death notice that appeared in the Honolulu Advertiser on September 24, 1925. It gives information on the date of death, place of death, and occupation of the deceased person. The word "sketch" means that there is an article that will give more information.

Slide 6: Marriage Index.

Slide 7: The Marriage Index is by island. Entries are in alphabetical order by the last names of both male and female parties. It gives either the date of marriage or the date when the marriage license was issued. It shows the names of the man and woman. The man's name is indicated by a (k). You may request the document by asking for the book and page number.

Slide 8: On the right is a marriage license application. Note that names of parents and place of residence are given.

Slide 9: Court Records Index: The indexes are arranged by island.

Slide 10: Probate Records: The Probate Index is arranged alphabetically by the person's last name. Look for the probate number and look up the records on the self-service microfilm.

Slide 11: This is an example of a Petition for Probate of Will. Josiah Dickens died in Honolulu in 1880. He left a personal estate consisting of notes and mortgages and other property valued at $75,000. When he died, his property was left to his wife and children. He drew up this will when he was 45 years old.

Slide 12: The Divorce Index is also arranged alphabetically by the person's last name. The (w) stands for wahine (woman) and the (k) stands for kane (man). Divorce records are also on microfilm.

Slide 13: This is an example of a divorce document. Kalani, the woman, is divorcing her husband on grounds of desertion and living with another woman by whom he had five children.

Slide 14: This is a close-up of a document.

Slide 15: The Equity Index is arranged alphabetically and is cross-indexed by the defendant's and plaintiff's names. Look for the case number and you may request the file with the yellow call slips.

Slide 16: The records should be read carefully for information on family relationships. In this family there are two children plus an adopted child, named Kekipi, who is a female, as shown by the "w" in parenthesis.

Slide 17: The Index to Wills is also arranged alphabetically. The copies of wills are on microfilm.

Slide 18: Wills should be carefully read for information that shows different kinds of relationships. In this example, Mr. Thomas was married to Maria who had a daughter whose last name was Silva. This suggests that Maria was previously married.

Slide 19: Census Records: See one of the State Archives' staff for a list of censuses available.

Slide 20: Census forms change, but in this example it gives information about occupation and place of birth.

Slide 21: It may also give the names of the people in the household, their ages, and the school their children attended.

Slide 22: City Directories: City Directories are found in the library, and can be very informative.

Slide 23: The City Directory is divided into island sections, and the names are listed alphabetically. It gives the name of the person, place of residence, and occupation.

Slide 24: It may give additional information on widows. Aki is the widow of Samuel.

Slide 25: It may also give a death date. Bettencourt died December 17, 1918 at age 77.

Slide 26: Tax Records: Tax records are kept by district. You may request them on the call slips.

Slide 27: Tax records show the amount of real property or land and personal property such as buildings or animals owned by a person. Also, because school, road, and poll taxes were paid by all males, all persons paying such taxes are listed.

Slide 28: Passenger Manifest: The Index to Passenger Manifests is located in catalog drawers with the yellow labels. The drawers are arranged alphabetically by nationality--mixed ethnic, Chinese, Japanese, Portuguese, and Russian. The cards within the drawers are then arranged alphabetically, usually by the first letter of the person's last name. However, many Chinese are recorded alphabetically by their given names; e.g., Ah Loy, Ah Sam, etc.

Slide 29: This is an index card for Lau Lai. It gives information on his age, sex, native country, date of arrival, the name of the ship, and his occupation.

Slide 30: This is an example of a Passenger Statement or Manifest. Note that Lau Lai's last place of residence was Honolulu. That indicates that he may have returned to China for a visit.

Slide 31: Naturalization Records: The Naturalization Index gives information on the date of naturalization and native country. Look for the volume and page number and then use the microfilm to locate your subject.

Slide 32: In this example, Mr. Wong, from China, residing on Molokai, became a citizen of the Hawaiian Islands on March 27, 1892.

Slide 33: The End.

The next set of slides is of various kinds of permits used by the Hawaiian Government to control the flow of Chinese to Hawaii. The information being presented is of a preliminary nature because research has not been completed.

Slide 34: Passports: The passport on the top was issued in Honolulu prior to departure for China. It was issued under the Foreign Office Regulation of March 25, 1884. It gives the name in English and Chinese and the place of residence in Hawaii.

The lower passport was issued by the Hawaiian Consul in Hong Kong to Chinese returning to Hawaii (probably those already in China at the time the Foreign Office Regulation of March 25, 1884 went into effect). It only shows the name of the bearer in English and Chinese. Act 27 of 1887 was an Act to Regulate Chinese Immigration; it required various permits to enter the country. Major revisions were made in 1890, 1892, and 1893 resulting in the use of more permits.

Slide 35: Applications and/or Permits to Enter the Kingdom: Early applications such as this include two photographs and an affidavit, frequently provided by his employer, attesting to the length of residency in Hawaii.

Slide 36: The Permit, issued before departure to China, gives the name, age, and occupation of the bearer, and the length and place of residence in Hawaii.

Slide 37: This is the reverse of the permit. It was signed and given a visa number by the Hawaiian Consul in Hong Kong. In this instance, there is a notation, "Permission is hereby granted to Yee Tong to take his brother's wife Ip She and two nieces." There are also remarks in Chinese. It is hoped that the State Archives can obtain some assistance in getting these translated.

Slide 38: The application for the permit was later standardized as shown on this form. In addition to name, age, occupation, place and length of residence, this form gives the name of the ship the applicant departed on. These were required by the laws restricting Chinese immigration passed in 1887 and 1888. You can gain access by the yellow Immigration Index or Register of Chinese Permits Issued.

Slide 39: Chinese Return Permit: The application for the permit gives the same information as the previous: name, age, occupation, length and place of residence. This application has the photograph posted on the application.

Slide 40: This application superseded the previous permit. It gives the same information and, in addition, the name of the ship and the date of arrival in Hawaii.

Slide 41: This slide shows the permit with the photograph attached so that it could be matched with the application. The reverse also has the signature of the Hawaiian Consul in Hong Kong and remarks in

Chinese. The Return Permits supersede the Enter Permits. Access is by index cards.

Slide 42: Applications for Special Permits for Chinese Minors to Enter the Kingdom: This allowed Chinese residents of Hawaii to bring in their minor children. The application shows name and residence of father, name and residence of mother, name and residence of child, and signature of the applicant, who was usually the father, and frequently in Chinese.

Access is by index cards of Registry of Chinese Minors. For earlier permits, see Enter Permits or Hong Kong Passports.

Slide 43: Special Certificate of Hawaiian-Born Children: This allowed Chinese children, then in residence in China, who were Hawaiian citizens by virtue of birth, to register with the Hawaiian Consul in Hong Kong. Being Hawaiian citizens, there was no time limitation on their return. The application shown and the permit to follow give name, age, and place of birth of child, name and residence of father, name and residence of mother, and name of the applicant.

Slide 44: This is what the permit looks like. Note the Chinese writing on the right. Sometimes such notations are on the back. Access is by index cards or Register of Hawaiian-Born Children of Chinese Parentage.

Slide 45: Women's Permits: The application was made to the Chinese Commercial Agent, who attested to the trustworthiness of the applicant, and referred it to the Foreign Office. The application usually gives the name and residence of the husband, and name and residence of the wife. In this instance, the woman is a daughter, so the names and residence of her parents are given.

Slide 46: Women's Permits were then issued by the Foreign Office. Such a permit gives the name of the woman and her place of residence and the name and residence of her husband or father. In this instance, there is a photograph with the application. Access is by index cards and Register of Chinese Women.

Slide 47: Special Certificate for Naturalized Chinese: These enabled the holder to be registered at the Hawaiian Consulate in Hong Kong as a Hawaiian citizen and to return to Hawaii without a time limit. It gives name and date of naturalization.

Slide 48: Conditional Permit for Chinese Clergymen, Teachers, and Colporteurs: This permit gives the name, age, place of residence of the traveller, his final destination in Hawaii, and his occupation. These permits were issued from 1893 through 1897.

Slide 49: Conditional Permit for Chinese Laborers and Domestics: These agreements between the laborer and the Foreign Office were an attempt to alleviate the shortage of agricultural labor and to prevent Chinese from entering as businessmen or tradesmen. Conditional Permits give name, residence, age, and signature in Chinese. On the reverse side, they were signed by the Hawaiian Consul at the port of departure, and sometimes have notations in Chinese. Conditional Labor Permits correlate with a Certificate of Identification which contains the photograph of the person. The Certificate of Identification also gives the name of the ship and date of arrival in Hawaii, and the name of the plantation to which the person was assigned.

Slide 50: This is a close-up of the Conditional Permit. Access is by index cards.

To comply with U.S. Immigration Laws, the last permits were issued in July, 1898, but those issued earlier were honored until the expiration date.

As I've mentioned before, these certificates and permits are being shown to give you an idea of the different sources of information available. The findings are preliminary, so we may not be able to answer some of your questions. The documents also need work done on them so that they can be handled safely, because some of them are in a very brittle condition.

Before closing, here are a few hints and reminders from the "Tools to Compile Your Family Tree" for happy hunting.

1. Check all variations of spelling and the reverse order of names.

2. Be flexible and be prepared to assess all pieces of information.

3. Read things carefully.

4. Take down your reference or where you got the information.

5. Take good notes.

6. Have patience, because the information you are looking for is not all in one place.

7. Concentrate on one step at a time so that you don't become distracted and side-tracked.

8. Be aware that record-keeping practices are not uniform.

9. Be aware that there are date limitations for written records.

10. Be aware that there are gaps in documentary sources.

HAWAII STATE ARCHIVES   (Start)   Tools to Compile Your
                                                  Family Tree Flow Chart

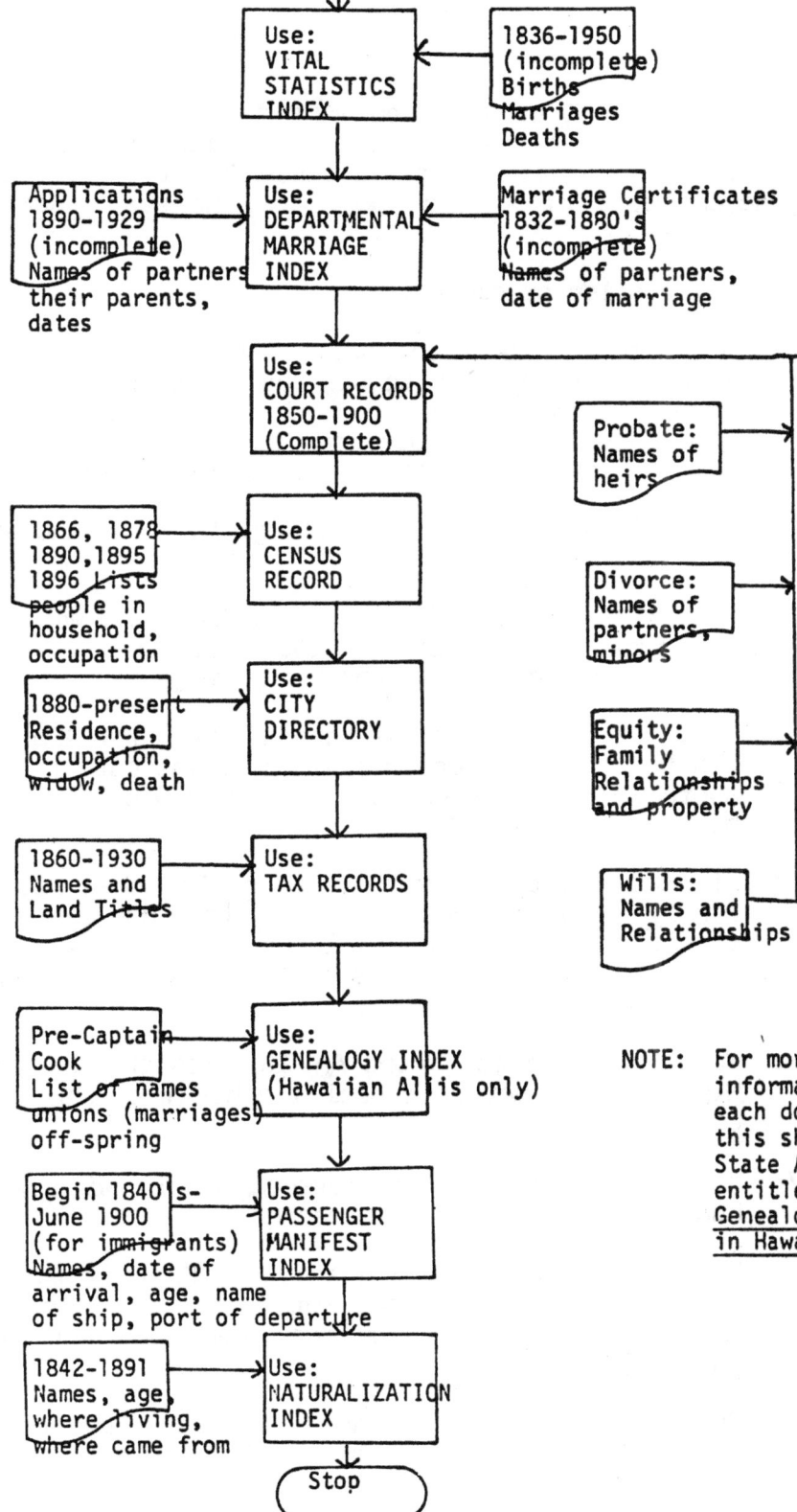

```
                              Use:                1836-1950
                              VITAL        <----  (incomplete)
                              STATISTICS          Births
                              INDEX              Marriages
                                                 Deaths

    Applications              Use:                Marriage Certificates
    1890-1929          --->   DEPARTMENTAL  <---  1832-1880's
    (incomplete)              MARRIAGE            (incomplete)
    Names of partners,        INDEX               Names of partners,
    their parents,                                date of marriage
    dates

                              Use:                        ┌──────────────┐
                              COURT RECORDS  <-------------│              │
                              1850-1900                    │   Probate:   │
                              (Complete)                   │   Names of   │--->
                                                           │   heirs      │
    1866, 1878                Use:
    1890,1895          --->   CENSUS
    1896 Lists               RECORD                        Divorce:
    people in                                              Names of       --->
    household,                                             partners,
    occupation                                             minors

    1880-present              Use:
    Residence,         --->   CITY                         Equity:
    occupation,              DIRECTORY                      Family          --->
    widow, death                                           Relationships
                                                           and property

    1860-1930                 Use:                          Wills:
    Names and          --->   TAX RECORDS                   Names and   ----┘
    Land Titles                                             Relationships

    Pre-Captain               Use:
    Cook               --->   GENEALOGY INDEX        NOTE:  For more detailed
    List of names            (Hawaiian Aliis only)         information about
    unions (marriages)                                     each document on
    off-spring                                             this sheet, read
                                                           State Archives' Pamphlet
    Begin 1840's-             Use:                          entitled: Searching
    June 1900          --->   PASSENGER                    Genealogical Records
    (for immigrants)         MANIFEST                      in Hawaii, 1982.
    Names, date of           INDEX
    arrival, age, name
    of ship, port of departure

    1842-1891                 Use:
    Names, age,        --->   NATURALIZATION
    where living,            INDEX
    where came from

                              ( Stop )
```

2/85

31

RESEARCH IN GENEALOGY FOR HE WAS A RAM

Violet Lau Lai

MOST OF YOU ARE HERE because you want to know how to trace your family tree. In your packet there is a "Mini Guide to Locating One's Chinese Roots." The nine points listed are those Kum Pui and I found most helpful in our seven years of work on our book, He Was a Ram: Wong Aloiau of Hawaii.

And now, a slide presentation:

Slide 1: Step one. Talk with your relatives. This could be your most important step. Ask to see their old photos, scrapbooks, family tree--anything. My relatives not only had information on genealogy, they had pictures to prove who belonged where in the family tree. Here are some of their pictures.

Slide 2: Wong Aloiau left Pun Sha Village in China and arrived in Hawaii in 1865.

Slide 3: His sponsor was Wong Kwai, a nephew, who was an important rice and sugar planter of the 1800s in Hawaii. Wong Kwai is the grandfather of Yan Sau and Bunny Wong.

Slide 4: This is Wong Feart, my grandfather and Aloiau's "Number One Son." Wong Feart early claimed he was born in China. Later, he swore in court he was born in Honolulu. A friend said, "Maybe he was born again!"

Slide 5: If Wong Feart was born in Honolulu, then his mother was most likely Hawaiian. Scientists say that one cannot tell a person's ethnic background by his looks. But my Uncle Solomon, on the left, Wong Feart's son, surely "looks" Hawaiian, and so do many of our relatives.

Slide 6: Wong Feart's wife, Young Ah Siu, was the daughter of Young Lai Him, the elementary school teacher who taught Sun Yat-sen in Choy Hang.

Slide 7: Ah Siu is expecting her eleventh child. With her is daughter Ah Lung who became a school teacher.

Slide 8: These are four of Ah Siu and Wong Feart's daughters. In front are Irene Wong Nagai and Ruth Wong Nip. In the back are Bow Ngun Wong Young and my mother, Alma Wong Lau. Aloiau's home is in the background.

Slide 9: We are now going to meet Aloiau's second family. This certificate reports the birth of Alice Miller. Alice's mother was Ellen Aloiau Wong, and Ellen's father was Wong Aloiau.

Slide 10: These sisters, Alice Miller Ohai and Sarah Miller, are Aloiau's granddaughters. I met Alice Ohai in 1980, and she remembered Wong Feart, whom she called "Uncle," as he used to bring her family food, clothes, and money.

Slide 11: The Alice Ohai family invited the Wong Aloiau clan to Kauai for a family reunion. Here is her family. See that blond boy in the front row? Because his family is interested in genealogy, he knows that Wong Aloiau is his great-great-great-grandfather. How many of you know who your triple great-grandfather is?

This same boy's ancestor, Meliaka Kunane, left Aloiau because she could not accept the Chinese double standard of fidelity. The <u>man</u> could date other women, but the <u>woman</u> had to stay at home. So she packed and left, even though she was pregnant with his daughter, Ellen.

Slide 12: Aloiau then married Emma Ellis, a Hawaiian-German girl of 14. This is Emma with their daughter, Rose, of Aloiau's third family. Emma was a lady of leisure. As a rich rice planter, Aloiau employed housemaids, and his plantation cook sent meals over. Like many Hawaiians, Emma was very sharing, much to her husband's annoyance. If a friend liked Emma's silk dress or her sandalwood fan, she'd say, "Take, take, I can always charge another one."

Slide 13: To curb Emma's extravagance, Aloiau bought ad space in a Chinese language newspaper, <u>Lung Kee Bow</u>, in 1889. This ad has genealogical significance because in it, he claims Emma as his wife. He also said, "To fellow Chinese storemen, to all who have given my wife credit: Please go chase after this Hawaiian woman. It doesn't affect me. Be warned to avoid future controversy."

However, Aloiau soon forgave Emma. That same year she gave birth to a <u>son</u>. But no one I interviewed could remember his name. Later, I found the boy's name in Aloiau's divorce court record, "Aloiau, Pake vs. Emma Aloiau." This is part of his divorce document.

Slide 15: Our family had assumed that his marriage to Emma was common-law, but the document said, "We were married in Papaa in April 1877, by the Rev. R. Puuki." Aloiau named the daughters Loke (Rose) and Amoe (Mollie), and his son, Elissa. I had found Elissa--the name needed for our family tree! You know, the day I found this information was the day I became "hooked" on researching the life of Wong Aloiau.

He blamed Emma for neglecting the sick baby, who died shortly. When she ran away to Honolulu...with her boyfriend...and refused to return, Aloiau sued Emma for divorce.

Now he had another problem. He needed a mother to care for the girls, Rose, age 7, and Mollie, only 3-1/2. He told the matchmaker he was through with Hawaiian women (you remember, two had run away). He asked for a healthy Chinese girl, one with natural feet. He considered bound feet a cruel custom which rendered a wife useless as a housekeeper.

Slide 16: So the matchmaker went to Ngai How Village and found just the right girl from the Tam Yuk Nam family. She was Mew Hin, the healthy second daughter who had natural feet.

Slide 17: With Aloiau's generous lisee, Mew Hin's parents bought her a new wardrobe, including this beautiful wedding skirt. Worn almost 100 years ago, the skirt is in excellent condition and will be exhibited at Kauai Museum this September.

Slide 18: Here is Mew Hin as a young wife with a Japanese girl, probably her maid. Later, Mew Hin had a big problem. After seven years of marriage, she had borne no child. When the Aloiaus hired a new housemaid, a miracle happened. Mew Hin became pregnant. The young maid, for bringing such good luck, was promoted to be a daughter, or "kai nee," and here is a family picture.

Slide 19: At left is the "kai nee," a Chinese hanai daughter. Mew Hin is carrying Vivian, her first child. Standing are Rose and Mollie, the part-Hawaiian girls, and here's Aloiau, about age 55.

Slide 20: Baby Vivian is now a teenager, with her status symbol--her own horse. With her is Clyde Kong, her nephew. Vivian found great favor with her parents, as they believed she "led in" her five brothers:

Slide 21: From left are Edwin, Ralph, Kenneth, Walter, and Godfrey Aloiau.

Slide 22: This photo of Aloiau and Mew Hin's family was taken around 1917 when Aloiau was 70 years old. This is his fourth family.

Slide 23: Now I'm going back to Emma's daughters, Rose Aloiau Kong and Mollie Aloiau Yap, who were school teachers. Some of you may have been their students.

Slide 24: Rose married En Sue Kong. Their children are from left, Clyde, Richard, and Daphne, now Apana. In back is Maurice.

Slide 25: Mollie, who married Alfred Yap, was the first exchange teacher from Hawaii to the Mainland in 1935. Their son, Harold "Dope" Yap, in 1931 was the first Hawaii boy to play in the Rose Bowl.

Slide 26: In 1917, Aloiau celebrated his 71st birthday, actually 70th, by the western calendar. He is surrounded by family members.

Slide 27: While you're interviewing your relatives, ask them about the different names of your ancestor, so that you can recognize these names in your research. We found ten different versions of Aloiau's name.

Slide 28: This display ad in Husted's Directory of 1880 carried the name "Ah Loy Yau." In the index of this same directory, his surname has become "Yau." His general store provided many services: selling, boarding house, even a Chinese laundry. Note the last three words: "Everything well cooked."

Slide 29: The family has two identical portraits, each carrying a different name. This one calls him "Wong Lo Yau."

Slide 30: Under this picture, his name is Wong Young Hong, the name acquired at marriage, or in Chinese his "gee miang" (字名   ).

Slide 31: At the See Dai Doo Society, the man in charge said that there was no one by the name of Wong Lo Yau registered. Yet later, the family found his membership certificate, under his honorific name, Wong Young Hong. It's dated 1915.

Slide 32: When you have a list of your ancestor's names, try locating him in the U.S. Census of 1900. This is one of the best sources to locate family history and genealogical information. Your ancestor may not have been in court, nor bought property, but he was most likely registered in the 1900 Census.

Slide 33: For example, we found the following information under the name "Ah Lo Yau." He was born in November 1846, had migrated from China in 1865, and spent 35 years in Hawaii. He could read and write, he could speak English, and he owned his home mortgage-free.

The same type of information is given for his wife, called "Tam Shee," and for his daughters, Yuen Sim (Vivian) and Amoy (Mollie), who were living at home.

Slide 34: Another good source to search is the State Department of Health, where you can apply for birth, marriage, and death certificates.

Slide 35: Earlier, I had pointed out Alice Miller's birth certificate which documented the name of her mother as Ellen Aloiau Wong.

Slide 36: The most important information on Aloiau's death certificate was the name of his father—Wong Hin Tai; this name would later link the family to an early genealogy record.

Slide 37: Another place to check is the tombstone.

Slide 38: Here the clan is visiting the Kapaa Chinese Cemetery, where Aloiau was originally buried. He was exhumed in 1931, according to his death certificate, and his bones transferred to the Lin Yee Chung Cemetery in Manoa.

Slide 39: The information on Aloiau's tombstone in Manoa is very valuable. In Chinese is the name of his village, Pun Sha of Chungshan District. Also given are two versions of his name—Lo Yau and

Young Hong.

However, the dates can be challenged, especially his death date --1920--carved in marble. His death certificate is dated 1919, and his obituary appeared on the front page of Garden Island, a newspaper, on August 19, 1919. How could he have died in 1920?

The point is that you cannot take only one record as the truth; you must check all available sources and then draw your conclusions.

Slide 40: Court records are another source.

I mentioned earlier that it was a divorce record that confirmed the legality of Aloiau's marriage to Emma. And that through this record, we found their son's name, Elissa.

Slide 41: Land documents can be a source for names of children and for Chinese characters of your ancestor's name.

Slide 42: You'll notice that this conveyance record is written in Hawaiian, the prevailing language during the days of the Kingdom. This lease is between Loyeau and Akawai. According to the Chinese calligraphy, probably copied by a Haole clerk, "Akawai" is really "Hee Kwai." This could be a good find for the Hee family. But "Loyeau" is missing a surname.

Slide 43: Next to the relatives, I found the tax records the most interesting source. They recorded about 50 years of Aloiau's assets--from nothing to his possessions as a "rice king" and landowner. For genealogical help, the tax records gave many versions of his name, and the names of his brothers and cousin who were living in Aloiau's store.

Slide 44: Older tax records in the Archives are very tedious to check. They are not indexed nor alphabetized before 1909. You just turn page after page until you find a listing that looks like it belongs to your relative. This is the first tax record of Aloiau I found. Called "Loiau, pake," he paid the minimum taxes of $5.00 in 1867 when he was poor and living in Waikiki.

Slide 45: If you're really serious about searching for your family tree, I'd like to recommend Jean Ohai's book, Chinese Genealogy and Family Book Guide: Hawaiian and Chinese Sources. If you are persistent, and will follow Jean's recommendations--as you would a recipe--your chances are good in tracking down your ancestors. Believe me, the work is tedious, but the rewards may be worth it.

Slide 46: Now, I'd like to share with you about a search for an older family record. I went to China in 1981 and made a detour to visit Pun Sha, Aloiau's village. This is Kwongchow, called Canton, where we left at 7:00 a.m. to travel south to Chungshan.

Slide 47: My cousin Kam Hoon and her husband Harry Lee were among the seven who made the trip. We had to make four river crossings by ferry. Here's one we just missed.

Slide 48: Pun Sha Village has probably changed little since Aloiau left it over 100 years ago. When I met my cousins who are descended from Aloiau's oldest brother, I immediately asked to see the "Ka Poo" (家譜) or family tree record.

"Mou lo! Siu sai lo" (冇咯！燒嘅咯), cousin said. He explained that during the Cultural Revolution, the villagers burned these family books. What a let-down that was!

Slide 49: While I was inwardly groaning, Harry Lee was busily snapping pictures. This former "chi tong" (祠堂), where the ancestral records used to be kept, is now a tool shed—gone to the dogs—or should I say, pigs.

Slide 50: However, that all-day trip was worth the effort. We took pictures of our cousins, and felt a warm kinship with them. These are third cousin Hong Ngew and his brother Shia Kai and their families. There's Kam Hoon in the back, and I'm barely visible at the right.

Slide 51: When I returned home, my China cousin sent me photos of the family's earlier houses. Still standing today is Aloiau's childhood home, which must be at least 140 years old. I also received the genealogy of Aloiau's brothers.

Slide 52: In Honolulu, third cousin Bunny Wong introduced me to fourth cousin Hong Hoy Wong. It pays to search out your relatives. Hong Hoy helped me write letters to my China cousins. He had been a recorder in Pun Sha, and he seems to know every relative in the village and most "Sam Wak Wongs" (王) in Hawaii.

One day, Hong Hoy phoned and said, "Biu Ja (表姐), are you still interested in the Ka Poo? I just found a copy in the trunk!" Wow! Kum Pui and I dashed down to the Hawaii Chinese History Center to meet him. He graciously lent me the family book, which his father had copied in 1931 before the originals were destroyed in the 1960s.

Slide 53: This is the cover to the "Ka Poo," or Family Record of the Wongs of Pun Sha. If you read Chinese, you can tell that it was copied in 1931.

Slide 54: The records go back to Sai Inn of Generation One; he had migrated from Tung Kun to Pun Sha around 1468. His ancestors were originally from Fukien. Fortunately, Aloiau and the owner of this precious book had identical ancestors up through Generation Eighteen.

Slide 55: Generation Nineteen consists of the five sons of Wong Uk Kwai.

Hong Hoy said that most "Sam Wak Wongs" of Hawaii are descended from one of these sons. The third son was Wong Hin Tai, the father of Aloiau! Remember earlier we had found Hin Tai's name on Aloiau's death certificate. Since this family book was copied for the descendants of the fifth brother, the names for Aloiau's clan had to be changed, beginning with Generation Twenty.

Slide 56: So our book, He Was a Ram, sponsored by the Hawaii Chinese History Center and the Wong Aloiau Association, went to the University of Hawaii Press with two genealogy charts. Larry Ing, who did the beautiful calligraphy on the cover, helped us add the names of Aloiau, his brothers, and his sons for the early Chinese chart.

Slide 57: I added a chart in English of all of Aloiau's known descendants. Being American-Chinese, I included the females, as well. This chart concluded with his great-great-great grandchildren, and here are a few who attended a family reunion.

Slide 58: Another reward, besides the accomplishment of putting out a book, was the bringing together of the four branches of the family. Formerly, we hardly recognized persons of another branch, but now we are one family. Here we are at a family reunion. We look forward to these get-togethers as we honor...

Slide 59: ...our beloved ancestor, Wong Aloiau. Thank you.

Seated are Mr. and Mrs. Wong Aloiau and Baby Vivian, c. 1900.
Standing l. to r. are Chun Hiu Inn, "kai nee," and part-Hawaiian daughters, Rose and Mollie, from a previous marriage.
(Courtesy of Daphne Kong Apana)

MINI GUIDE TO LOCATING ONE'S CHINESE ROOTS   By Violet Lau Lai

1. <u>Talk to relatives</u> and neighbors of ancestor. See their photos, scrapbooks, correspondence, etc.

2. <u>Check for the various names</u> your ancestor was known by. For example, Wong Aloiau was also known as Loiau, Ah Loy Yau, Wong Young Hong (his honorific name acquired at marriage). This "married name" is on his tombstone, portrait, See Dai Doo membership card, and on the family genealogy chart. Verify the name(s), especially the surname in Chinese characters. You may find these characters on land documents, correspondence, or on the tombstone.

3. <u>Check the U.S. Census of 1900.</u> Ask for help at the Hawaiian Room, Public Library, main branch. The Census is organized by island and district, and usually family members are listed under the male head of household. You may find the following information in the Census:

    a. Year of birth
    b. Year of arrival from China
    c. Occupation
    d. Whether he could read and write, or speak English
    e. Name of wife and number of years married
    f. Names and birthdates of children and of others living in the same house

4. <u>Apply for Birth, Marriage, and Death Certificates</u> at Department of Health (fee). The certificates may contain the following information:

    a. Dates of birth and death
    b. Place of birth
    c. Names of parents
    d. Place of burial
    e. Information on exhumation

5. <u>Check tombstone,</u> which may give--

    a. Name in English and Chinese. Chinese name may be his "married name."
    b. His district and province of China.
    c. Dates of birth and death.

6. <u>Check older court records</u> at Archives. Ask where more recent records are kept.

7. <u>Check land records</u> at State Conveyances Division. Search through indexes to Grantee Records and Grantor Records by island.

8. <u>Check tax records</u> at State Archives. More recent records are kept in the Circuit Court.

9. <u>Read Jean Ohai's book,</u> CHINESE GENEALOGY AND FAMILY BOOK GUIDE. Book is available at the Hawaii Chinese History Center.

CHINESE SURNAMES IN HAWAII

Irma Tam Soong

FROM YIP WANG LAW and Wai Jane Char we have learned that to identify accurately the character for your Chinese surname is the first step toward doing your genealogy.

Researchers into the Chinese characters for Chinese-sounding surnames will find that English spellings vary in Hawaii as greatly as they do in all parts of the world where there are overseas Chinese.

The reason is that China did not have a nationally accepted phonetic transcription of the Chinese language until 1919. Such a system is needed for pronouncing words. In 1921 Mandarin was declared the national language or kuo yu of China. However, the phonetic transcription was slow to be accepted in a country with poor communication and beset by problems of adjustment to a modern world. Besides, it was not romanized. It is only since the rise of the People's Republic of China that kuo yu has taken a firm hold on the Mainland. It is called putong hua (p'u t'ung hua) and is anybody's version of kuo yu. And pinyin is now the authorized system of romanization. An example of putong hua would be speaking Mandarin with a Cantonese accent. An example of pinyin romanization is Beijing for Peking, Xian for Sian.

A national system of romanization and a national spoken language have helped to unify China, which was linguistically unified before this by the written language only. Before this, romanizations of dialects were attempted by Christian missionaries and by anyone who needed an English equivalent of a Chinese character. Hakka suk wa is an example of a missionary-originated alphabetized system to transcribe the Bible and Bible lessons into a readable Hakka version. Hakkas were able to write letters to each other in this romanized Hakka dialect.

As for western Sinologists, the most widely used system of romanization was the Wade-Giles system. It has been a great spur to western studies of Chinese history, language, and literature. It has been used in library card cataloguing up to the present. An example is Teng, which in pinyin is spelled Deng, while T'eng would be spelled Teng.

In Hawaii, Mandarin was unknown to the early immigrants who came mainly from South China. Therefore, their surnames reflected their dialectal backgrounds and were romanized by the English speller to the best of his or her ability. For example, the surname 謝 is spelled in at least ten different ways: Char, Dea, Dere, Dare, Dair, Jair, Jea, Tse, Hsieh, Jay, and Sia.

Besides the problem of dialectal differences and the lack of a widely accepted national language in the early days, the Chinese presented a unique problem to his western host. His surname came first and was often mistaken for a given name. Thus his Chinese surname was sometimes lost if it was not recorded in some form. For example, in the full name of Deng Xiao Ping, Deng, his surname, comes first. If he were a resident of early Hawaii, he might have gone by the surname of Ping or Ah Ping.

Tracing a Hawaiian-Chinese surname to its progenitor is therefore a very difficult task in many cases. Generally speaking, however, if we know the name of the village or district of the immigrant ancestor, we can make a start.

The Punti Dialect

The bulk of the earliest immigrants came from Chungshan County, then called Heungshan. The Heungshan dialect, or Punti, is a rural version of the prestigious Cantonese that is spoken in Hong Kong and in Canton. Yet in Heungshan itself there are Hakkas and speakers of Nam Long, Lung Doo, and Sam Heong, too.

In Chungshan the county seat is Shekki. It boasts of a Heungshan dialect that is more "refined" than that spoken by the inhabitants of the rest of the county. For instance, "eat" is spoken as "yak," "hiak," or "suck." The Shekki Chinese would say "sake," as in "for goodness sake." It is the same way Hong Kong Chinese would say "eat."

The Fukien Influence

The three dialects, Nam Long, Lung Doo, and Sam Heong are variants of Min dialects. The ancestors of these speakers had sojourned in the Min River area of Fukien Province before they moved down south to Kwangtung and therefore had absorbed the Min dialects into their own. Because Taiwan natives are originally Fukienese as are many Chinese in Southeast Asia, all these people can understand each other to an extent.

41

The Hakka Dialect

As for the Hakkas, they come not only from Heungshan and speak Heungshan as well, but come also from districts adjoining Kowloon, in, around, and north of Canton like Fayuan, Tsingyuan, and Muiyuan. Their dialect, according to Tin-Yuke Char's research, is "a combination of Peking vowels, Foochow diphthongs, Canton finals, and Hankow tones."

Sam Yup, See Yup Dialect

Besides these main groups, we have in Hawaii immigrants from Sam Yup and See Yup Counties. The Sam Yup dialect is like Cantonese. Most Sam Yup immigrants settled on the U.S. Mainland rather than in Hawaii. Some See Yup settled in Hawaii. Their dialect has a distinctive characteristic that can be traced back to their sojourn in Fukien.

Multiple Names

Every historian doing research on the biographies of Chinese is confronted many a time with several given names for one individual. These may be a milk name, school name, marriage name, professional name, and others. A generation character is a helpful guide to the generation of a person in his clan. There usually is a set of words, one for each generation. For example, Sun Yat-sen and his brother, Sun Mi, both had Duck 德 in their marriage names. One was Duck Ming and the other Duck Cheong.

To assist the researcher, two lists of surnames are attached to this presentation. The first is designed to facilitate finding the Chinese character for a surname that is spelled in English. It is based primarily on a list compiled by Donald K.F. Ching, with changes by Kum Pui Lai. The second is a list of Hawaiian-Chinese surnames found mainly in the Oahu Telephone Directory of 1985.

In the first list, no attempt has been made to add the pinyin equivalents, as they are not in wide use among the Chinese here at this conference.

Hawaiian-Chinese Surnames

Genealogical research for those with Hawaiian-Chinese surnames is a field all its own. The early plantation laborers were registered under their given names rather than their full names. Without a Chinese surname listed, the researcher has to ask relatives, copy gravestone markings, check baptismal records and society records for clues. A surname might be lost also when a young Chinese lad entering school for the first time was asked his name and was registered with his surname as his given name and vice versa. Thus, the children of Tom Ah Loy became known as the Ah Loy family. Surnames like Lum-King and Chun Hoon are a parent's full name carried on as a family surname. The surname "Wo" is the second character of the given name of C. S. Wo, whose full name was Ching Sing Wo.

Chinese words are monosyllabic. Most Chinese surnames are single characters. A few are composed of two characters, e.g., Auyong, Seto. Given names, on the contrary, are usually composed of two characters, e.g., Kam Sing. But they may be just one, e.g., Sing. In both cases, Kam Sing or Sing might be addressed as Ah Sing in speech.

Many Hawaiian-sounding surnames are not true Hawaiian names. Furthermore, these surnames are not Chinese surnames either. They are Chinese first names with "Ah" or the prefix "A" 阿 , 亞 before it. They are informal given names, relationship names, or Hawaiianized Chinese given names used as surnames.

The prefix "A" or the word "Ah" is a diminutive like "ette" in the French name Jeanette or the "ie" or "y" in the English name Jimmie or Johnny. Such names are informal names used by family and friends. A Chinese example would be Ah Lan instead of Yuk Lan, and Afook instead of Kam Fook. Afook, Asing, and Ah Loy are examples of first names used as Hawaiian surnames.

Sometimes Hawaiian-Chinese surnames were originally family relationship names like Apo, meaning "grandma," Ako, meaning "elder brother," or Ah Nee, meaning "No. 2 child in the family." Chinese like to address family friends, not only their true blood relatives, by affectionate appellations denoting close family relationships.

Often a Chinese will take on a Hawaiianized first name like Akana, which is derived from "A" plus "kan" plus "a" with its soft Hawaiian suffix, as his surname. Other Hawaiianized Chinese surnames are Ahana, Awana, and Ai.

These coinages were evidence of the warm relationship existing between the native Hawaiians and the early Chinese immigrants. Many Chinese spoke Hawaiian as their second language, and many Hawaiians went to China with their Chinese husbands or fathers and spoke Chinese fluently. The intermarriage of Chinese men with Hawaiian women and the Chinese effort to adapt themselves to their Hawaii environment account in a great part for the many Hawaiian-Chinese surnames that can be found in the Oahu Telephone Directory today.

CHINESE SURNAMES IN HAWAII

Compiled by Irma Tam Soong [This list is based on an article, "Chinese Names," written by Donald K.F. Ching, assisted by Kum Pui Lai, and printed by the Hawaii Chinese History Center.]

AU 歐

AUYONG 歐陽

CHAI 瞿

CHAN 陳詹

CHANG 鄭 張

CHAO 趙

CHAR 謝

CHAU 周

CHEE 徐

CHEN 陳

CH'EN 陳岑

CHENG 鄭 程

CH'ENG 程

CHEONG CHEUNG 張

CHEW 周

CHEY 趙

CHIANG 江

CHIEN 簡

CH'IEN 錢

CHIN 陳

CHING 程 陳

CHINN 錢 陳

CHO CHOCK 卓

CHOI 蔡

CHONG 張

CHOU CHOW 周

CHOY 蔡

CHU CH'U 朱 周

CHUCK 瞿

CHUEY CHUI 徐

CHUN 陳

CHUNG 鍾 程 張

DAIR 謝

DANG 鄧

DARE DEA DERE 謝

DONG 曾

DOO 杜

DUNG 鄧

ENG 伍吳

FANG 方

FENG 馮

FO 賀

FONG 方 馮 鄺

45

FU	胡	
FUNG	馮 鄺	
GAN	簡	
GEE	朱 甄	
GIN	甄	
GO	高	
GOCK GOK	郭	
GON	簡	
GONG	江	
GOO	古	
GOON	阮	
GOONG	龔	
GUM	甘	
GWOK	郭	
HALL	何	
HAN	韓 侯	
HAU		

HE	何	
HEAU	邱	
HEE	許	
HEU HEW HIU	邱	
HO	何 侯 賀	
HOH	何	
HOM	譚	
HON	韓	
HONG	洪 唐 熊 湯 康	
HOO	胡	
HOW	侯	
HSIAO	蕭	
HSIEH	謝 薛	
HSIUNG	熊	
HSU	徐 許	
HU	胡 黃	
HUANG		

HUEI HUEY HUI	許 譚 馮	
HUM	譚 洪	
HUNG	洪 邱	
HYAU	伍 吳	
ING	袁	
IN INN	葉	
IP	葉	
JAIR	謝	
JANG	鄭	
JAY JEA	謝 甄	
JEN	甄	
JEU	趙	
JEUNG	張 周	
JEW	趙 詹	
JIM	詹	
JIN	甄	

46

JOE	周			
JONE	鐘			
JONG	張 周 趙			
JOW				
JUE				
JUNG	張 曾			
KAN	簡 康			
KANG	孔			
KAO	高			
KAU				
KIANG	江			
KO	高			
KONG	江 鄺			
KU	古			
KUAN	關			
KUANG	鄺			
KUM	甘			
KUNG	孔 龔			

KUO	郭
KWAN	關
KWOCK	郭
KWOK	
KWONG	鄺
LAI	賴 黎
LAM	林
LAU	劉
LAW	羅
LAY	利 黎
LEAU	廖
LEE	李 利 呂
LEI	李 雷
LEM	林
LEN	連
LENG	淩
LEO	廖
LEONG	梁

LEU	劉
LEUNG	梁
LEW	劉
LI	李 利 黎
LIANG	梁
LIAO	廖
LIEN	連
LIM	林
LIN	林 連
LING	淩
LIU	劉 廖
LO	駱 羅
LOCK	駱
LOH	羅 駱
LOK	陸 羅
LOO	盧 陸
LOOK	
LOOY	呂

47

LOR	羅	MAU	毛	NGOON	阮	
LOUI LOUIE LOUIS	雷	MEI	梅	NIEH NIP	聶	
LOW	羅	MEW MIAO MIU	繆	ONG	任 吳	鄧
LU	陸 盧	MO	莫	OU OW	歐	
LÜ	呂	MOCK	莫 莫	麥		
LUEY	呂 雷	MOI	梅	OUYANG OUYONG OWYONG OWYOUNG O'YOUNG	歐 陽	
LUI LUIE	雷	MOK MORK	莫			
LUK LUKE	陸	MOO	巫	PAN P'AN	潘	
LUM	林	MOU	繆	PANG	彭	
LYAU	廖	MOW	毛	PEI	貝	
MA MAH	馬	MOY	梅 繆	P'ENG PONG	彭 潘	
MAI MAK	麥	MU		POON	潘 馮	
MAO	毛 馬	MUEY MUI	梅	POONG		
MAR MARR	馬	MUN	文	QUAN	關 郭	
MARK	麥	NEEP	聶	QUOCK	郭	
		NG	任 吳	QUON	關	

SEE	施 薛	**SIU**	蕭	**TENG** **TENN**	鄧		
SEID	薛	**SO** **SOO**	蘇	**THOM**	譚 鄧		
SEN	孫	**SOO HOO**	司 徒	**TIEN** **TING**	譚		
SETO	司 徒	**SOON**	孫	**TOM**	唐 湯		
SHAM	岑	**SOONG**	宋	**TONG**			
SHEE	施	**SU**	蘇	**TOY** **TS'AI**	蔡 曾		
SHEM	岑	**SUE**	蘇 蕭	**TSANG**	謝		
SHEN	沈	**SUEN**	孫	**TSE**	曾		
SHEW	蕭	**SUM**	沈 岑	**TSENG**	鄒		
SHI **SHIH**	施	**SUN**	孫	**TSEU** **TSOU**	徐		
SHIM	沈	**SUNG**	宋	**TSUI**			
SHINN	車 成	**SZETO** **SZUT'U**	司 徒	**TU**	杜		
SHUM	岑			**TYAU**			
SI	施	**TAAM** **TAM**	譚	**UNG**	伍 吳 鄧		
SIA	謝	**TAN**	譚	**VON**	溫		
SIEW	蕭	**T'AN**	譚	**WAN**	溫		
SIN	孫	**TANG**	唐 湯 鄧				
SIT	薛	**T'ANG**	唐 湯				

49

WANG	王	YEH	葉
WAT	屈	YEM	嚴
WEE WEI	衛	YEN	袁 嚴
WEN	溫	YEONG	楊 葉
WENG	翁	YEP	嚴 葉
WEY	衛	YIM	嚴
WON	溫	YIP	葉
WONG	王 黄	YONG YOUNG	楊 容
WOO	胡	YU	余 俞 阮
WOON	溫	YUAN	袁 俞 容
WU	胡	YUE	余 阮
WUN	溫	YUEN	袁 余 翁
YAN	甄	YUNG	袁 曾
YANG	楊	ZANE ZEN	曾
YAP	葉		
YAU	邱		
YEE	余 俞		

THIS MORNING'S LECTURES have provided us with an understanding of the importance of identifying one's Chinese surname by its Chinese character as a start to doing one's genealogy or family history.

And we are beginning to see how difficult genealogical research is to do just because China was not unified in speech and had not earlier accepted a uniform romanization of Chinese words. The many dialects and variant spellings are confusing. Also, the fact that the Chinese surname precedes the given name has turned many given names into surnames in Hawaii so that some surnames are lost forever. Then there is the Chinese custom of having many names.

Here are some suggestions for starting your family history.

For those of you who happen to know the Chinese character for your surname, you are fortunate. You can proceed from there. If you don't, where can you find it? Jean Ohai's <u>Chinese Genealogy and Family Book Guide: Hawaiian and Chinese Sources</u> contains one of the best summaries of the problems one faces and sources to pursue in Hawaii.

Briefly, I would like to point out those sources you can begin with:

1) Old family records like immigration and citizenship papers, obituaries, letters, certificates of birth, marriage and death, etc.

2) Photographs which identify the persons and which record the date and place or occasion.

3) Cemetery records and gravestone markings.

4) Society listings, church records.

5) Interviews with relatives and friends.

Sometimes you can find a family genealogy book or a clan genealogy book. The University of Hawaii's Asian Collection has some clan genealogies. The Mormon Church's genealogical libraries are a great help. You may have to write back to your village to see if a family genealogy exists. Or you may inquire about this on your visit to the village. Since not many of us can read Chinese, some persons at the Hawaii Chinese History Center can suggest Chinese scholars who can assist you. We hope that someday all the clan genealogies will be translated into English. If the demand is great, it will be done.

Now, if you have done all the work on documentary material that you possibly can, perhaps you would like to do not just your genealogy, but a readable family history that your children will find enjoyable and valuable.

For this, you must continue to interview. Always keep a notebook handy. Take down notes every time a person has the time to tell you something—during a meal, at a party, on a visit, on the bus—anywhere. Note the date and the place. Be curious and be a good listener. Ask questions about everyday life, food, clothing, housing, occupations, hours of work, festival times, relationships with family members and the community, religious affiliations, communication, transportation, financial problems, language, adjustment to Hawaii, etc.

If the person you interview is not too old to tape-record, find a quiet room and have your questions ready. Be sure to record the name of the person, the date, and the place on the tape before you begin or after you have finished for the day.

After you have done your background history, you might want to write about your own life. Work out a brief outline—chronologically from birth, through childhood experiences, schooling, work, marriage, etc.

Write a rough draft. Never mind about your grammar and spelling. Your own expression is sometimes the most colorful. Later on, your writing can be edited with someone's help.

Gather your photographs and label them. Collect documents. These can be duplicated and the copies used with your rough draft.

If you still can't begin to write, try to recall the most memorable events in your life. Was a certain event happy, hilarious, tragic, critical? How did you meet crises? What in your background determined the way you reacted?

Do you have a philosophy of life? What keeps you going every day? Is religion important to you? If not, why not? What makes you happiest? What would you like to tell your children? Perhaps they aren't interested today, but one day they will be and will be grateful to you for leaving behind your wisdom to guide them.

The last page of Jean Ohai's paper, the blue sheet, has many, many suggestions of topics for you to write about. It is entitled, "Suggestions and Items to Consider in Writing Your Personal History."

HAWAIIAN-CHINESE SURNAMES

Compiled by Irma Tam Soong

ABING	ALO	AH CHONG	AH PING
AFOOK	ALOIAU	AH CHOY	AH QUIN
AHANA	AMANA	AH COOK	AH SAM
AHI	AMONA	AH FONG	AH SAN
AHINA	AMONG	AH HEE	AH SEE
AHOA	AMOY	AH HO	AH SING, AHSING
AHU	APANA	AH HOU	AH SIU
AHUE	APO	AH HOY	AH SOON
AHUNA	APUNA	AH KEE	AH SUE
AI	ASAM	AH KING	AH SUI
AIU	ASAO	AH LEONG	AH TOU
AKAKA	ASING	AH LO	AH TUCK
AKANA	AWA	AH LOO	AH TYE
AKAO	AWAI	AH LOY	AH VAN
AKAU	AWANA	AH MAI	AH WONG
AKEE	AYAT	AH MAU	AH YAT
AKI	AYAU	AH MOI	AH YEN
AKINA		AH MOO	AH YO
AKIONA	AH CHAN	AH MOOK	AH YOU
AKO	AH CHEONG	AH MOW	AH YUEN
AKUI	AH CHICK	AH NEE	AH YUN
ALANA	AH CHIN	AH NEW	
ALINA	AH CHING	AH NIN	

CHINESE NAMES IN HAWAII

Wai Jane Char

DURING AN EVENING three weeks ago, a television spot called "Mixed Plate" showed a Chinese family gathered together in celebration. They had found their roots! Daniel CHING, who had researched his family lineage, spoke. An aunt was introduced as Mrs. CHINN. Also introduced was a paternal uncle who had come from China for this special occasion. He was introduced as Mr. CHEN.

Interestingly, they actually have the same surname, written 陳 . Because of dialectal and other differences, this surname is pronounced and romanized as follows: in the Punti dialect this surname is pronounced Chun; in Hakka, the dialect of Daniel's family, it is Ching; his uncle took the Mandarin romanization and called himself, Chen, according to the Wade-Giles system of romanization. Wade and Giles, missionaries to China, established a system of romanization. Today the People's Republic of China is promoting the pinyin phonetic system and its version would be spelled Chen.

The Daniel Ching family used the dialect of the Hakka. Who are the Hakka? Centuries ago in North China a group of Chinese settled as "guests" in an already occupied area, probably Honan. Through the centuries they kept their customs, traditions, and speech--the Hakka dialect. In migrations they went east, west and mostly south.

We, here in Hawaii, are concerned with the peoples of Kwangtung. This province is the place of origin of most of the immigrants to America. To South China they had gone in waves of migration, escaping floods, famines, dynastic changes, and other disturbances. Many settled in other provinces like Fukien before making their way into Kwangtung. Their speech took on some Hokkien dialectal patterns--noticeably in Lung Doo and Nam Long patois.

Migrants came into Kwangtung over mountains through Nan Ling Pass and by sea. The Hakka settled in East River areas--Meihsien, Waichow, some parts of Tungkun, and Pao On, which included Kowloon and Hong Kong. Daniel Ching's father left Waichow for Hawaii.

The Hakka are part of the Chinese race who generally are called Han

Chinese, <u>Hon Yan</u> (漢 人), after the great Han Dynasty (206-219 A.D.). In Hawaii, as in Kwangtung, we also speak of ourselves as Men of Tang, or <u>Tong Yan</u> (唐人), after the glorious Tang Dynasty (618-960 A.D.). A majority of people moving into Kwangtung moved into the areas of Sam Yup (三邑), Chungshan (中山), Sze Yup (四邑) which were delta and choice farm lands. Migrations of Hakka and non-Hakka occurred about the same time; greatest influxes were during the Sung (宋) Dynasty (960-1197 A.D.) when Mongolian hordes invaded China.

The groups reaching the delta areas first, especially the Chungshan people, called themselves Punti or "locals." The use of the term Punti was singularly a local Chungshan usage. It does not mean, in this instance, native or indigenous people.

Chungshan people, as well as those of Sam Yup, Sze Yup, and the Hakka, had distinct dialects with many sub-dialects, all too numerous to mention here. This resulted in a variety of English spellings.

To illustrate the differences in speech, let's go back to the name CHING. When a Sam Yup or Chungshan person says CHING, he means the last name 程 . This is the surname of the Punaluu CHINGS, Hung Wo CHING, or Achuck 程直 , who was a well-respected Chinese merchant working together with CHUN Afong during Monarchy days. Achuck's descendants include Silva, Ordenstein, Kauhini, Medeiros, Ahue, Olds, Napoleon, Sumner and others, according to John Topolinski and Mrs. Irma Agard, genealogy researchers.

CHING 程 is also pronounced in some dialects in Hawaii as CHUNG. But C-H-U-N-G in English may also be pronounced CHOONG which stands for the character 鐘 , last name of Lawrence K.C. CHUNG who is known for kung fu and lion and dragon dances of Chinatown. We see C-H-U-N-G used in this name CHUNG-Hoon 張寬 , ancestor of William CHUNG-Hoon, Sr. and Jr., Rear Admiral Gordon CHUNG-Hoon, the Awai, Rosehill families, and others. In Chungshan dialect, we pronounce this C-H-U-N-G as Jeong, and the character is written 張 . It is also spelled C-H-O-N-G as in last name of the late "Me, P.Y. CHONG" of restaurant fame. And it is the last name of the president of the Hawaii Chinese History Center, Douglas CHONG.

Also, there are two names that sound alike in Southern Chinese -- 黃 (yellow) and 王 (lord or chief). Wong 黃 (yellow) is last name for Richard Wong, president of Hawaii's State Senate. Wong (lord) is the last name of Wong Aloiau, <u>He Was a Ram</u>, a new book to be discussed by author Violet Lai today.

Therefore, it is important to find out the Chinese character for one's last name or <u>sing</u> (姓), as well as the place of origin or ancestral home in Kwangtung <u>ngyuen jick</u> (原籍). A given name is called <u>ming</u> (名).

How can one find one's Chinese last name? Gravestones are revealing. Not only do some provide in carved Chinese characters the birthplace of the deceased, but also the full name, usually with surname preceding the given name. Some will even include the honorific name acquired at marriage, called <u>dai jee</u> (大字), the name used in the family genealogical book.

A married woman's name is commonly written with her maiden surname followed by <u>Shih</u> or <u>Shee</u> or <u>See</u>. For example, your grandmother may have been known as <u>Tam Shee</u>, which means she is a married woman who came from the Tam clan.

Documents in archival libraries and government offices are invaluable sources for names. Mrs. Peggy Kai was researching the ancestry of her husband, Judge Ernest Kai, when she found his Chinese great-grandfather's signature 鄧行善 (TANG Hung Sin). Tang and some contemporaries were "sugar masters" from China. They were active around the 1840s, as they milled sugar for Hawaiian kings or governors, for foreign adventurers, or for their own plantations. Peggy learned the names of nearly all six or seven "sugar masters" who were, incidentally, mentioned in a 1929 bilingual annual, <u>Chinese in Hawaii</u>, published by the Overseas Penman Club. My husband, Tin-Yuke, and I assisted her with the research and Chinese words.

The most important source for your own family history is the book called, <u>gar poo</u> (家譜), a family genealogy or register, or generation book. Many early families sent information on children born in Hawaii to the village ancestral halls for recording. Or, your grandfather, or great-grandfather may have kept a small record book for Hawaii-born additions to the family book.

You may also locate ancestors in a clan genealogy like the modern one of California, <u>Chu Clan Condensed History</u> (趙族簡史). Many such family genealogies and clan genealogies have been collected in the Mormon Church's granite vault in the Rockies. Large university libraries in the United States, including Hawaii, as well as Hong Kong and Taiwan, have smaller collections.

Whenever you find your name, copy it, and someone who knows Chinese can rewrite it for you.

And so we find our link to the past--to family, to clan, to China's rich history and traditions. Identity is important to boost feelings of belonging.

CHINESE SURNAME SOCIETIES IN HAWAII AND RECORDS OF ONE'S GENEALOGY

Wallace W. Y. Wong

TODAY'S WORKSHOP has been sponsored by the Hawaii Chinese History Center in the hope that you may become more interested in your beginnings and learn a little more about how you may trace your family's beginnings. This organization has played an active part in tracking down data about the early Chinese immigrants, making records, and, more recently, sponsoring a drive to get oral records from older folks who can recall their youthful days.

I have been asked to share with you my knowledge about the surname societies in Hawaii and how to go about finding records of one's ancestors here and in China. My experiences as vice-president and president in 1982 and 1983 of the Chinese Chamber of Commerce afforded me opportunities to learn of the work of the surname societies. I am the first to admit that I am not an expert, and fortunately was able to find resource books and resource persons such as Mr. Welton Won of the Chinese Chamber of Commerce.

First, I shall briefly touch upon some historical aspects that have influenced the development of surnames. Going back to the "Five Emperors Period," there were originally only 22 surnames. Emperor titles were Wong Dai, Jean Yook, Dai Goong, Dai Yew, and Dai Sun. Moving ahead to the Han Dynasty (200 B.C. to 220 A.D.), China now had 127 surnames. During the Tang Dynasty (618-907 A.D.), called the Golden Age of Chinese Culture, this number increased to 1,913, and by the Yuan Dynasty (1271 to 1368) under the great Kublai Khan, there were 3,736 surnames. When China became united in the Ming Dynasty (1368-1644) under Chinese rule, there were 4,657 surnames.

HOW WERE SURNAMES ARRIVED AT? First, the surname could have been given by the emperor, lord, marquis, earl, or some other high-ranking official. Second, the surname could be the birthplace of that person. Third, the surname could be a variation of a given name through mispronunciation, and fourth, a surname could be changed as a penalty for violating the law.

The first example tells how the surname Chong came into being. The fifth son of the Yellow Emperor was named Ah Fai; he invented the bow and arrow. It was so helpful in battle that the Emperor decreed that Ah Fai should bear a new surname, that of Chong. The written character has the figure of a bow on the left, and the right side has an ideograph meaning "long." Together, the word Chong 張 connotes that the bearer of this name would have many children. Women looked favorably on a marriage into this family. In 1940 or thereabouts, the surname Chong was said to be the most frequently used name among the Chinese.

A second example is one incident in the troubled conditions during the Chin Dynasty (221-207 B.C.). Members of the Han clan were fleeing from Emperor Chin's troops. The Chin leader confronted the Han leader, and demanded his name. The answer was, "We are Hon people" (the word meaning "cold"). The Chin leader thought he had heard Ho, meaning river. So the Ho's are originally Han.

A third example is the alteration of a surname. An emperor of the Wei Dynasty (220 A.D.) by the name On Doong Wong disliked a high official whose surname was Yuen 元 . Because he violated a law, the emperor figuratively cut off his head by removing a stroke from his name; the resulting word is pronounced "nguk," meaning alone and written as 兀 . In 1915, at which time the population of China was 400 million, the five most common surnames were Chun 陳 , Lee 李 , Wong 黃 , Chong 張 , and Ho 何 , followed by Au 歐 , Chow 周 , Hu 胡 , Ma 馬 , and Mark 麥 .

Here I should like to explain that the Chinese who came to the islands were mostly from the provinces of Kwangtung and Fukien. These two provinces are on the coast way down south. They are 1,600 miles from Peking and 800 miles from Nanking. The influence of foreigners was strong. The Portuguese were allowed to stay at Macao as early as 1519. The port of Canton was open to foreign trade, primarily with the British, Portuguese, and Dutch, who all flourished. The need for labor in Hawaii was publicized in the port areas, so thousands came to Hawaii as contract laborers. The contracts set down wages, length of contract, and health and welfare arrangements for the migrants. To those struggling with a bare existence in China, this presented a chance to lift themselves from poverty.

Many Hakka people answered the call for labor. They came from the areas near Hong Kong, such as Kowloon, New Territories, and from towns like Shatin, Pukak, and Lilong. This group had moved during the Chien Lung period (1736-1795) seeking better land and opportunities. An organization for people who spoke the Hakka dialect was first organized in San Francisco, when Tong wars were going on. The original name, Yin Fo Society, meaning people in harmony, was later changed to Tsung Tsin Society for the Hakkas.

Most of the other migrants were described as Punti, meaning local to the land, but much rivalry surfaced so that they were not too hospitable to the Hakka or guest people. The Puntis are generally the immigrants from Heong Shan area. Heong Shan later became known as Chung Shan, in honor of Dr. Sun Yat-sen. More than 75% of the Chinese living here are descendants of migrants from the Chung Shan district. Looking at this map of Kwangtung may enable you to see the locations. The Pearl River winds its way, and on the other sides are the North River, West River, and East River. Mountains also created barriers causing separation and isolation.

This map shows the location of ten "doos." Starting at the northeast there is Larm Doo, slightly below is Lung Doo and Leong Doo, Yun Doo with Duck Doo to the northeast, and See Dai Doo bordering on the Pearl River. Further south and bordering on the China Sea are Gook Doo, Kung Seong Doo and Wong Leong Doo. Notice that Shekki is the county seat of Chung Shan. In spite of the dialectal differences of different groups, the dialect spoken in Shekki became the standard speech of the Chinese inhabitants in Hawaii.

See Yup people speak another subdialectal speech; they came from Toy Shan, Yan Ping, Hoi Ping, and Sun Wui, while Sam Yup people came from Pun Yu, Shun Tak and Nam Hoi. They are located a little closer to Canton and therefore their dialect is closer to the official dialect spoken in the capital city of Kwangtung.

Looking at another map of Kwangtung, you can notice that the population was centered in the Pearl River delta area near the coast. Fukien is its neighbor to the northeast with Swatow as a port, and the Nan Ling Mountains act as a barrier to its north. Kiangsi province and Hunan province are to the north, with Kwangsi province to the west.

When the early Chinese immigrants first came to Hawaii, many were lonesome in these strange Sandalwood Islands. They sought companionship and help when they needed it. They sought out other immigrants from their native village or district in China.

Village and district clubs were not the only clubs of the Chinese in Hawaii. Those of the same political belief formed clubs; those of the same type of jobs organized. Surname clubs were also formed.

AREA FROM WHICH MOST CHINESE IN HAWAII EMIGRATED

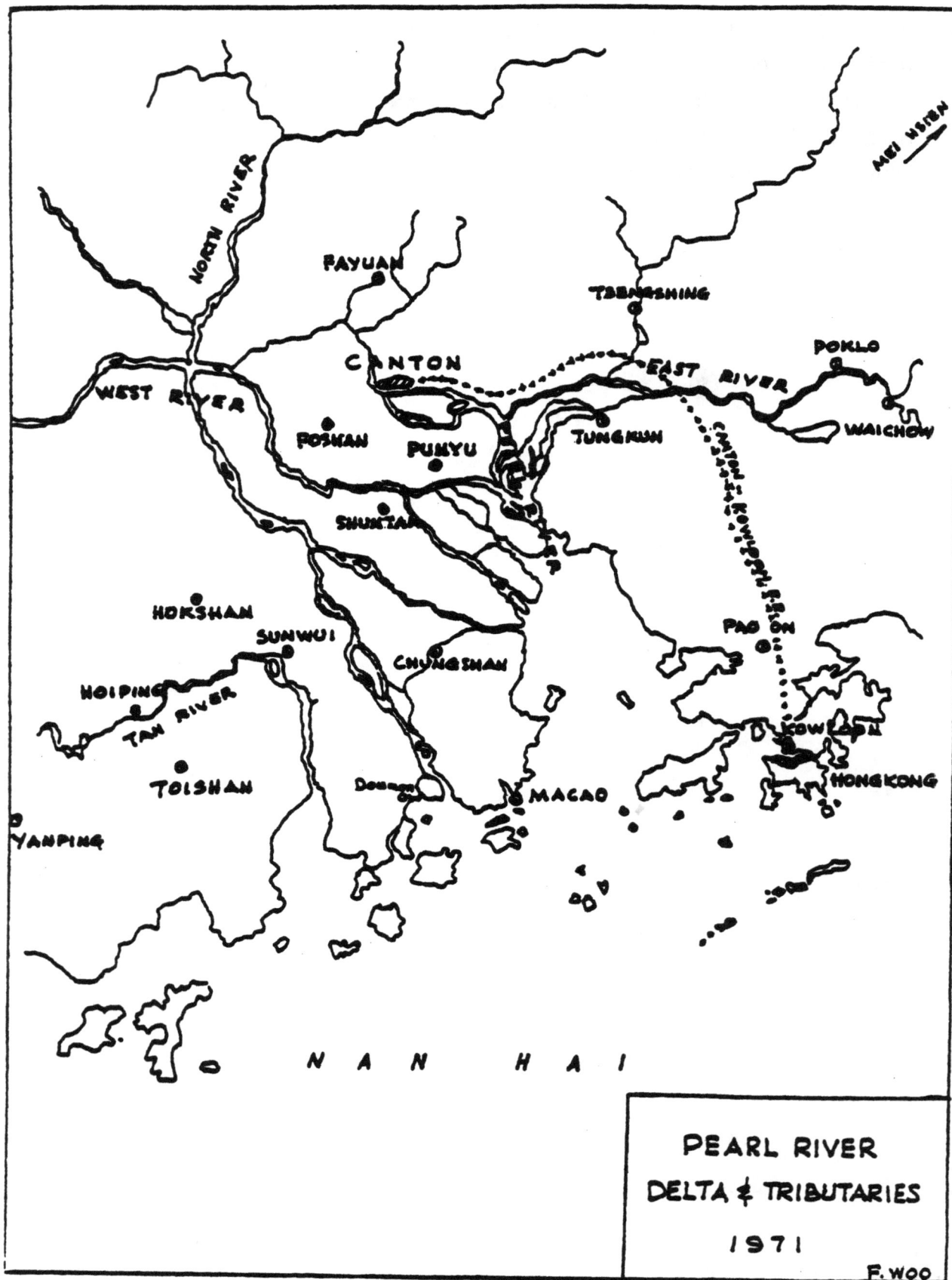

MEI HSIEN

NORTH RIVER

FAYUAN

TSENGSHING

CANTON

POKLO

WEST RIVER

FOSHAN

PUNYU

TUNGKUN

EAST RIVER

WAICHOW

CANTON-KOWLOON R.R.

HOKSHAN

SHUNTAK

PAO ON

SUNWUI

CHUNGSHAN

HOIPING

KOWLOON

TAM RIVER

HONGKONG

TOISHAN

Doumen

MACAO

YANPING

N A N   H A I

PEARL RIVER
DELTA & TRIBUTARIES
1971

F. WOO

CHINESE SURNAME SOCIETIES IN HAWAII WITH DATES OF ORGANIZATION

CHANG WING YONG TONG, 1956 鄭榮陽堂

GOO ASSOCIATION, 1954 古氏同宗會

CHING BENEVOLENT SOCIETY OF HAWAII, 1957 程氏同宗會

CHUN WING CHIN TONG, 1959 陳穎川堂

HEE GOW YONG TONG OF HAWAII, 1961 許高陽堂

HO SOCIETY OF HAWAII, 1939 何氏宗親會

ING COUSINS CLUB, 1963 吳氏宗親會

KAM SOCIETY, 1929 甘氏同宗會

LAU FAMILY ASSOCIATION, 1980 劉氏宗親會

LEE ASSOCIATION, 1954 李氏宗親會

LEONG SOONG DUCK TONG, 1915 梁崇德堂

LOUI SEE FAMILY SOCIETY, 1963 雷氏同宗會

LUKES OF HAWAII, 1963 陸氏宗親會

LUM SAI HO TONG, 1889 林西河堂

MA'S CLANSMEN ASSOCIATION OF HAWAII, 1915 夏咸走馬氏宗親會

MAU CLUB OF HAWAII, 1931 毛氏同宗會

SIU SOCIETY, 1982 蕭氏宗親會

TOM ASSOCIATION, 1950 譚氏宗親會

WONG KONG HAR TONG, 1902 黃江夏堂

WONG MUNG DUCK TONG, 1980 王明德堂

YOUNG ASSOCIATION, 1952 楊清白堂

LUNG KONG KUNG SHO, 1919 龍岡公所

    aka SOCIETY OF FOUR FAMILIES:
    LAU, QUON, CHONG, AND CHU 劉關張趙

THE VARIOUS SOCIETIES were organized in Hawaii to do charity work, to settle disputes, to raise money for educational needs, to assist with famine and flood relief, and to keep the members close together. The following are among some of the larger societies:

Lum Sai Ho Tong was established in Honolulu in 1889. Headquartered at 1315 River Street, this group was founded to foster fellowship among the Hawaii families with the surname of Lum, Lam, Lim, or Lin. It conducts Chinese rituals and worship in Tin Hau Temple, which houses the Ku Po goddess. This society has traced its ancestry to Prince Pi-Kan, prime minister of King Chao in the later years of the Shang Dynasty (1766-1122 B.C.). The Shang Dynasty was also called Yin Dynasty because its capital was at Yin and remained there till the end of the dynasty. The tyrannical ruler, King Chao, in a fit of anger, killed Pi-Kan who had the audacity to admonish him. His widow fled into the forest, and in a stone cave her son was born. His family name became Lim or Lum, meaning forest.

Lung Kong Kung Sho Association is one of the largest and best-known international organizations. It had its beginnings during the period of the Three Kingdoms (201 A.D.) when Lau Pei, Kwan Yu, and Chong Fei swore themselves to brotherhood with a Peach Orchard Pact. Chu Wun was later admitted as the fourth sworn brother. The story of the struggles between the three contender warriors--Tsao Tsao, Sien Chuan, and Lau Pei--are kept alive through popular novels and plays. The Hawaii Chapter was formed in 1919 with its present headquarters located at 1432 Liliha Street. Lung Kong also has a physical culture club.

Wong Kong Har Tong Society was organized in Hawaii in 1902. The character Wong may be written with three cross strokes, or written to mean yellow 黃 . The Yellow Emperor gave the name Kong Har to an area of Honan province in northern China, and its members use the character Wong, meaning yellow. This group gives scholarships to deserving members of the Wong clan, and also aims to promote educational, benevolent, and charitable activities.

Incidentally, I discovered that Taiwan has a strong Wong surname society. In June 1975, I was invited to Taiwan by the Taiwan government along with 24 delegates from the United States. The Wong Society hearing that two delegates had the surname Wong, invited them to their own party although the entire delegation was being entertained by the Kwong Tong

Tung Heong Hui that same evening. In 1976 a delegation of 35 Wongs from Taiwan passed through Honolulu on their way to Sacramento. The local Wong Society entertained with a dinner and was presented with a large tapestry depicting the eight immortals and also a distinguished banner of silk showing the characters Wong Kong Har Tong Society.

The Tung Sin Tong, organized by the Sam Yup group in 1885, elected a family to lead and serve for one year. They set up a cemetery in Pauoa instead of a clubhouse. They met four times a year, collected funds to clean the grave area, and provided food for the get-togethers. This was open only to Sam Yup families.

The See Yup Benevolent Society was organized in 1897. They had a clubhouse and did charitable projects. Yi Yee Tong was an organization for See Yup people and provided for physical training of males. Also Kong Chau Society is a group which is restricted to See Yup people only from the Sun Wui district.

Lung Doo Benevolent Society had headquarters on Aala Street between Beretania and Kukui Streets. They have a large membership, own buildings which bring in rent, and is considered to be one of the wealthier societies. One of its purposes is to exhume the bones from local cemeteries after five years and ship the bones to China for reburial. They have facilities for the destitute and carry on charity work, hold reunions, and settle disputes.

VILLAGE CLUBS

Oo Sack Kee Loo, for the people of Oo Sack Village, Gook Doo, was organized in 1897. It owns a clubhouse at Kamakila Lane.

On Tong Villagers' Club, for the people of On Tong Village, Lung Doo, was organized in November 1926.

Lungtauwan Villagers' Club, for the people of Lungtauwan Village, Lung Doo, was organized in February 1926.

Wai Bok Say is a club for the people of Cha Yuen village of See Doo. It was organized in 1927.

Siu Yun Quon Chark Say, organized in 1921 by and for the people of Siu Yun village in See Doo. It has no clubhouse. It is inactive now.

Buck Toy Villagers' Club, for the people of Buck Toy village in Leong Doo. It has a clubhouse on North Vineyard Street.

Yung Wo Tong, for the people of Yung Mark village in Gook Doo, could be considered inactive.

TRADE GUILDS

The United Chinese Labor Association was organized in August 1917 by Kuomingtang members. Membership includes students, agricultural workers, merchants, educators, businessmen, government officials, accountants, engineers, doctors, lawyers, and many others. It is not a labor union as we understand it today. Its primary purpose is to promote the welfare of members, create employment, render aid to the sick and destitute, and to promote fellowship among members. It has no labor leader and it does not represent the laborers.

Seong Gah Hong, or Carpenters' Guild, was formed about 40 years ago. Its original headquarters was on River Street near Vineyard.

Wing Lok Ngue Hong, or Fish Dealers' Guild, was formed in 1903; is perhaps the most active among the guilds. This guild has rental property.

The Chinese Butchers' Association is also called the Ngow Yuk Hong. It was formed in 1928 with original headquarters on the corner of Hotel and Maunakea Streets, located on the second floor.

Hoy On Tong is an organization for Chinese people working on ships. It was founded in February 1903. Its headquarters were somewhere in Chinatown. Except for the annual election, it would be considered inactive.

Quon On Kwock, an organization for cooks and waiters in hotels and restaurants, was organized in August 1901. Most of the members have changed their occupations since then and not much is known about this association.

Gut Hing Kung So is for musicians and actors. Founded in May 1922, it is still very active.

Tan Sing Dramatic Club is also for musicians and actors. Founded in 1926, it is still in operation but is not very active as a guild.

Wah Hing Tong or Laundrymen's Guild, Bark Yee Hong or Dressmakers' Guild, Gum Yee Hong or Tailors' Guild, and the Luen Hing Club or Waiters' Guild were organized by the local Chinese, but all of them have ceased functioning due to lack of interest among the former members.

NOW I SHOULD LIKE TO MOVE AHEAD to discuss how one may proceed in the quest for one's genealogy. First, you must reaffirm your surname and find the character used to designate it. Wong may be a three-stroke word 王 , or a character meaning yellow 黄 . Next, check on your close relatives to find any information relevant to your quest. Some uncles and aunties are excellent sources of information, and they may have photographs, letters, and family records which provide clues.

Or you may check with the appropriate surname society for information about others who have been successful in their search. You must also find out the name of the village, the particular district and sub-district. Some people have been successful in confirming information by going to the State Archives to look for records of arrivals from the Orient or for citizenship records, and at the Department of Health for birth, marriage, and death records.

SOME DIFFICULTIES in finding your real surname may come from the way the plantations preferred to keep their records. The worker was listed by his name; for example, Ching Man became Amana, Lau Chiu became Achiu, so that some given names such as Ah Loy, Akina, Ako, Akao, Ahana, Ah Nee, and Ah Fong were accepted by the later generation as surnames.

Another difficulty came as a result of intermarriages. The males were separated from their legal wives in China. If they married a Hawaiian woman, the information about the man's ancestral tree was often lost. Also, in cases when the father remarried after the death of his first wife, the family records were often lost or destroyed.

In the traditional close-knit Chinese family of the old days, each head of a household kept a copy of the family tree which went back many generations. The great-grandfather, his brothers, unmarried sisters, the children, grandchildren, and great-grandchildren were listed. The family record was updated every 25 years, and the manuscript was wrapped and hidden in a safe place. The name for it is Chia Pu (家譜).

Interestingly, male cousins frequently used a common middle name. This helps to distinguish the generation level. The males carry a common qualifier, and often the female children used another qualifier. For instance, my middle name is Won 允 , and my three brothers also have Won in their names. Girls often use Kum meaning golden or Mei for beautiful. I had the experience in the 1930s to visit in Shanghai. An uncle from my village called together the relatives to meet me. At the banquet, I was amazed to meet twelve so-called cousins, and they all had the same middle name as I. This indicated that we had a common ancestor and that we were of the same generation, and that they came from Nam Hoi

Inn in Kwang Tung province.

This qualifier word may also be the third character in the complete name. For instance, in the Doo family, the sons all carry the word Chow-- Mee Chow, Sai Chow, and Kwai Chow.

SOME INFORMATION ABOUT THE NAM LONG DISTRICT. If the surname was Au, the village he left when he moved to Hawaii was probably "Chow Boo Tau". This village also had many families with surnames Fong, Yuen, and Sun. Chun families would have been from "Char In" village; Lum families were from "Siu Yun," and Wongs 王 would be from "Boon Sa" village in See Dai Doo. Originally, these Wongs came from Honan province from an ancient locale called Tai Yuen, situated between Sian and Peking.

Lee surnames could be Chinese from Lung Doo and See Dai Doo. Wong families (yellow) 黃 may have come from Leong Doo, Lung Doo or from Sam Yup. These Wongs from Heong Shan came there by way of Fukien to Kwang Tung. They are descendants of Mai Shee Tai Po 米氏太婆 , a matriarch bearing the name Mai or Mei.

In summing up this presentation, historians agree that the cradle of Chinese civilization was in the Huang Ho or Yellow River area, comprising of Shan Sai, Ho Nam, Shim Sai and Shan Tung. Recurring floods made life difficult and migration began to the south toward Fukien, and later to the southernmost province Kwangtung. Some groups moved to Taiwan.

THE CHINESE RACE represents an assimilation of a number of racial strains, of which the Han (漢族) predominated. The five colors of the Chinese flag--red, yellow, blue, white, and black--represent the five Chinese nationalities, that of the Han, Moon, Mong, Hui (Sinkiang), and Jong (Tibet). Other minority groups were the Turki, Tung Hu, and Miao racial stocks. Huang Ti, a distinguished leader, came into power 46 centuries ago; his reign marked the beginning of recorded Chinese history. Although Kwangtung was not considered highly civilized until the Tang Dynasty (618-907 A.D.), it was at Canton at the beginning of the sixteenth century that the East and West met. The Kwangtung people were the first to do business with Westerners. This early exposure prepared this province to adopt western ideas and modes of living. The adventurous people in Fukien and Kwangtung went outside to different parts of the world to work, to settle, to make new lives.

To conclude, I might venture to say "Lucky we come Hawaii," but the main point of today's workshop is to get you more interested in your ancestors and your background, and we hope that you will actively seek to find your genealogy, because now you are more aware of your roots. Thank you for your interest in joining this discussion.

THE ENIGMA OF CHINESE NAMES

Lawrence W. Ing

PLACEMENT OF THE SURNAME in a Chinese name puzzles many foreigners. To add to the confusion are the number of Chinese surnames and the many names given to an individual during his lifetime.

As to the number of Chinese surnames, there are 408 single and 30 double surnames recorded in the Pai Chia Hsing, or the Hundred Family Names, of which the most common are Wang, Chang, and Li. There were over 9,000 surnames, according to another source.

The Chinese surname comes first, as in the telephone directory, to be followed by the given name.

About one month after the child is born, a feast is given and he is endowed with a milk name, yue ming 乳名 , which entitles him to be recognized in society for the first time. This event closely corresponds to a christening when a child is received into the church.

A new name is bestowed upon him when he enters school, which is called shu ming 書名 , or hawk ming 學名 , which consists of two characters reflecting upon the condition, prospects, studies, or some other event connected with him. He is addressed by this title by his teacher and schoolmates, in official matters, and in anything concerned with literature.

When a young man gets married, two more names are added to his collection of names. One is his style or great name tze 字 , which his parents and relatives use in addition to his milk name. For acquaintances and friends outside of the family circle, another name called the hao 號 is adopted. These follow the surname, but since the Chinese have many contacts with foreigners, the order is sometimes reversed and the western practice of converting the hao into initials is adopted. Some examples are T. V. Soong, C. T. Wong, and V. K. Ting.

Local examples are--

C. S. Wo: His surname is Ching, and his personal name is Sing Wo.

C. K. Ai: His surname is Chung, and his personal name is Kun Ai.

Here are other examples of converting personal or given names to surnames: William N. K. Chang's surname is Ng (or Ing); now his surname

70

is part of his personal name. The same goes for Philip Ng Sing whose Chinese personal name is Yau Sing. N. K. Young's surname is also Ng; his personal name is Kam Young. Alfred Apaka's original surname is Lau; his Chinese given name is Fat.

By checking your surname, it is possible to tell whether you belong to Punti, Hakka, See Yup, or another group. These are examples:

Tai Yau Chung: His surname in Punti is Ching;
the Hakka version is Chung.

Larry F. C. Ching: His surname in Punti is Chun;
his Hakka version is Ching.

Thomas T. Y. Chung: His surname in Punti is Chong;
his See Yup version is Chung.

Sometimes a family adds an extra consonant to its surname; e.g., Richard TONGG from Tong; Mary Ann CHANGG from Chang; LAMM from Lam.

Many surnames used by persons of various dialects complicate matters also. On the mainland U.S.A. and Canada, there are such names as Gow, Der, Owyang, Meu, Jew, Seid, Ip, Gock, Tsoi, Chyr, Dair, Jang, Wy Roh, Jau, and Kwee.

Painstaking time is required to decipher these names and to find out their equivalent in the Cantonese version. They could be assumed names or aliases. My own surname Ing is also known as Ng, Ung, Wu, Woo, Go, Ngo, and Ngor. The Oscar winner Haing Ngor has the same surname as mine. So, to be certain, always ask for the Chinese written character, if possible.

All Wongs are not the same. Those who spell their name as Wang are "the three stroke" Wongs 王 . And those who call themselves Huang are "the big stomach" Wongs 黃 . However, there were [in 1985] 1,372 Wongs in the telephone book, and no one can tell for sure which "Wong" these persons are until one knows their particular Chinese character.

In the old days, every scholar assumed one or more "studio" names, peih hao 別號 , and officials on taking a degree or entering into government service added an official name, kuan ming 官名 , to their other means of identification.

After death, he was known by a posthumous name, shih hao 諡號 , inscribed on his tablet in the Hall of Ancestors. The deceased of the imperial family were provided with a temple name, miao hao 廟號 , and it is by these that past emperors are always referred to. These temple names can usually be translated as the lofty, virtuous, or exalted ancestor. The ruler's name during his lifetime was completely taboo, and only the reign title, which had nothing to do with the individual occupying the throne, described the period of his control. The sovereign personal name was regarded as so sacred that no one was permitted to utter, write, or make use of a phrase which vaguely resembled it as long as the same family remained on the throne, even after the death of the monarch who bore it.

This type of taboo is further carried on in that it is not considered proper for a child to have his own parent's personal name which implies disrespect.

The nomenclature of girls is much more simple than that for their brothers, as they are reduced to a milk name, a marriage name, and nicknames. After the wedding, a woman retains her maiden surname and is only addressed by her husband's surname through courtesy. In official documents her two surnames are combined. For example, a Chang girl who is married into the Li clan would be designated as Li Chang Shih. The last character indicates that Chang was her maiden surname. The chun ming 郡 名 , or territorial appellation, is hardly ever used except for girls on their marriage documents.

A further complication is introduced by the use of tang ming 堂名 , or family hall names, in some cases. The characters are generally inscribed in one of the principal rooms of the mansion, and are used on tombstones and in legal deeds.

The multiplicity of names describing any individual is undoubtedly confusing to the foreigner, but in his relations with his Chinese friends, only his clan name or surname is of importance for direct intercourse.

FAMILY HISTORY VIA VIDEOTAPE

Reported by Kum Pui Lai

ROSEMARY TONGG CHUN demonstrated the effectiveness of the videotape as a vehicle to portray family history in today's modern, electronic age. She described the collaboration of her family and the experts to produce a video using color and sound to depict the highlights of her father's career in creating beautiful landscapes.

Richard C. Tongg, called the "dean of Hawaii's landscape architects," started humbly at fourteen as the janitor and groundskeeper at Hilo High School. Besides his spectacular overnight planting of ten coconut trees, each thirty feet tall, on Bishop Street, he was responsible for the design and planting of many landscapes, among them the gardens of Honolulu International Airport, Pearlridge Shopping Center, Paradise Park, Andrews Amphitheater, and Kona Shopping Village.

The video, featured on television in San Francisco and in Honolulu's Spectrum, complimented Tongg's genius as a landscape artist in connection with his work on the Maui Hyatt Regency Hotel. The video was produced in 1984 in honor of Tongg's 85th birthday.

"Researching One's Chinese Roots" attracts more than 400
persons to McKinley High School in Honolulu on July 27, 1985.

Right: At the registration desk, Helen Ing, Marilyn Ching, and Allison Takinishi are
well organized to pass out registration packets to attendees who arrive en masse.

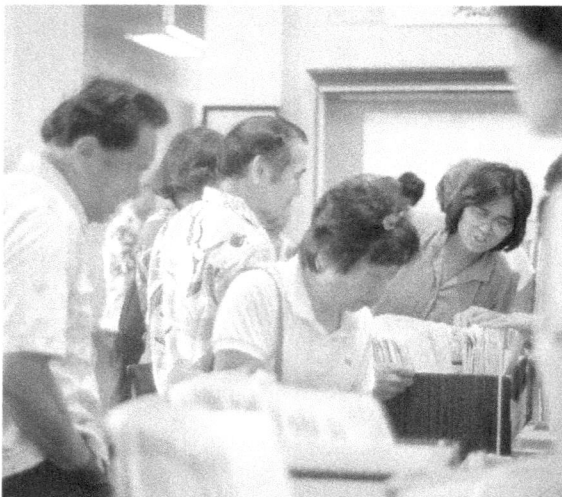

Encouraged by husband, Tin-
Yuke, Wai Jane Char works
on her presentations.

"Early birds" are Kam Man Leong, Hung Dau Ching,
Thomas Chung, and Dorothy Ako. Tommy will later
videotape the Conference for future viewing.

Puanani Kini Woo, center, executive director
of Hawaii Chinese History Center, and Conference chair, Richard Kam, and Kuulei Punua.

Hung Sum Nip shows a map of his early Chinese
neighbors of Upper Fort Street of the 1920s
through the 1930s.

Wallace Wong, center, speaker on Hawaii's Chinese Societies, with Marsha Hee and Roger Hee.

Speaker Violet Lai checks "Research in Genealogy for He Was a Ram."

Left: Irma Tam Soong, executive director emeritus of Hawaii Chinese History Center, discusses the Hawaiian influence on "Chinese Surnames in Hawaii." Right: Choy Wun Chang shares her experience in "The Chinese of Waipahu" with interested conferees.

Left: Helen Hu Wong, discussion leader, describes living conditions in "Tin Can Alley." Right: K. P. Lai recalls the delicious surplus "jook" doled out after 10:00 p.m. from Lee Buck Ngin's small soup eating place.

Larry Ching, center, founding president of Hawaii Chinese History Center, Thalia Choy, and Vivian Young.

Wah Chan Ching talks about "The Chinese of Punaluu."

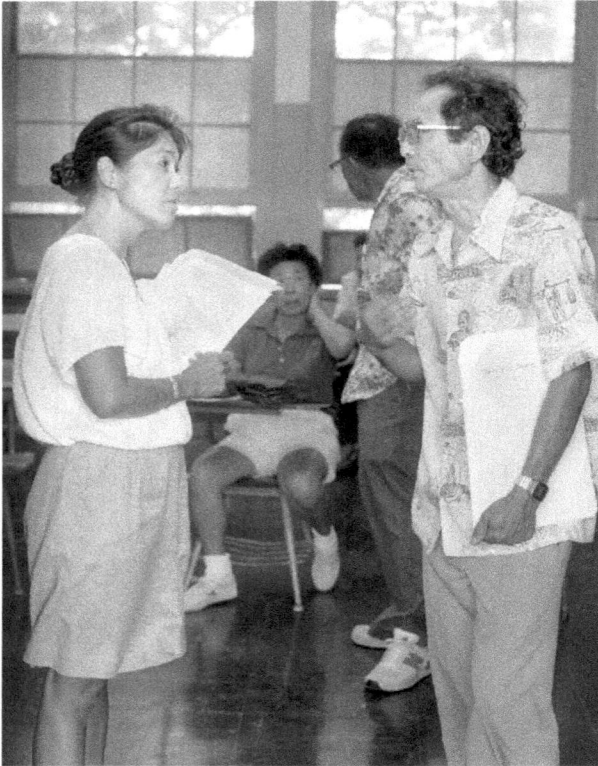

Cousins Lee Myers and Gary Chang com-
pare notes on their common heritage.

Yip-Wang Law traces the development of names through usage in
"The Origin of Chinese Surnames."

Right: Douglas Chong faces a roomful of persons interested in his advice
and experience in "Locating One's Ancestral Village." Chong was president
of HCHC in 1985 and 1986.

Left: Mary Ann Akao, archivist at the Hawaii State Archives, checks genealogical sources for her talk. Right: Toy Len Chang takes copious notes.

Ben Kau, Kum Pui Lai, and Norma Lum relax after a worth-
while day. Norma served five years as secretary of HCHC.

Lunchtime was a welcome break between the morning presentations and the afternoon group sessions. Below left: Fred Young, a "Distinguished Lion," serves punch. Below right: Speakers Fred Mau of Maui and Albert "Papa" Like and wife Bessie receive their Chinese box lunches.

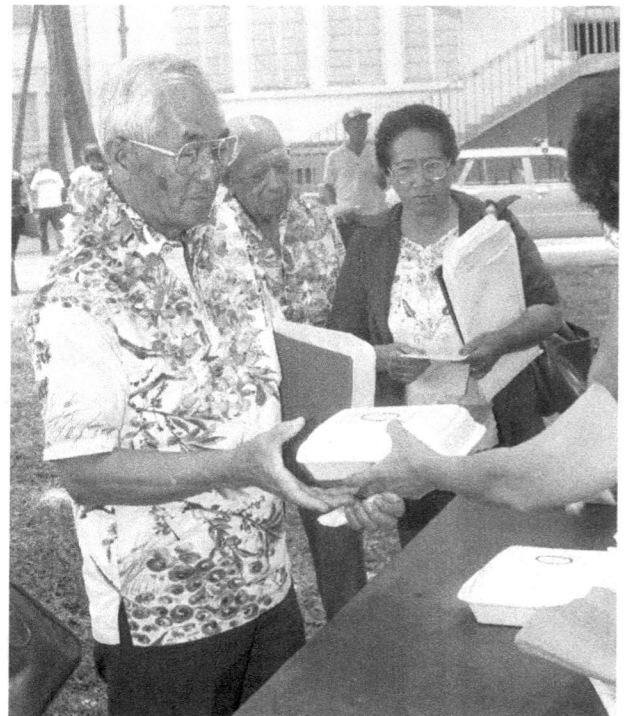

CHINESE SETTLEMENTS IN HAWAII

EARLY CHINESE IN HILO

Wai Jane Char

I AM SORRY that our scheduled speaker Peggy Kai is ill. With the help of Albert Like, an Hawaiian authority, I shall do my best to fill in for her.

I shall be quoting extensively from Peggy Kai's research and writings about the Chinese of Hilo. She wrote in the Journal of Hawaiian History (1974) that even before the coming of the first Chinese contract sugar laborers in 1852, there was already another group of Chinese settlers in Hilo. They were the sugar manufacturers, or sugar masters, called "tong see" (糖師) described in the Chinese language section of Chinese in Hawaii (1929) which Tin-Yuke Char pointed out and translated for Mrs. Kai.

"These sugar masters all married Hawaiian women, in some cases women of very high rank. They became citizens of the Kingdom of Hawaii, and melded into the community to a greater extent than some of the other Chinese." Chinese marrying Christian Hawaiian women were asked to become Christians, also. In addition, "the sugar masters became landowners and included their Hawaiian wives in their business dealings," she wrote. "The inclusion of the wives in official documents has made the identification of these Chinese settlers more certain; Hawaiian women's names were peculiarly their own at this period, and few shared the same name."

The Chinese names of the men in the group were Hawaiianized and the Hawaiian names so replaced their Chinese names that the knowledge of their original Chinese surnames was lost by many descendants. In the research I was doing, I had identified many of the early Chinese, and Peggy matched them to their Hawaiian wives. In many documents, Hawaiianized names were followed by these names written in Chinese characters.

Among the Chinese whom Peggy researched was Aiko, or LUM Jo 林佐. Records show that Aiko, an ambitious businessman, while primarily interested in sugar, also chartered ships, owned a store and a bowling alley, and bought, sold and leased property in Hilo. He was born in China and died in Hilo in 1895 at age 95. A convert to Catholicism, he was buried in the Roman Catholic Cemetery. In 1839, he was at Iole, North Kohala in partnership with Hapai, or Lau Fai (劉輝), in milling sugar. Later, the two men appeared to be operating the Hilo Sugar Plantation at Ponohawaii on the hill above Hilo.

Aiko appeared to be the trusted leader among his group. When Ahsam (a baker who worked at the location of what is today's Financial Plaza on Fort Street Mall) drowned in Honolulu Harbor on August 4, 1847, his widow, Ana Kamakohema, legalized the guardianship of son Akana to Aiko. In my article in the same Journal of Hawaiian History mentioned earlier, I had a full account of Ahsam and his partner Amau who were bakers in Honolulu.

Aiko and his Hawaiian wife, Maria Kaahuapea, seemed to have had only one child, Amelia Akoi, but Aiko served as a guardian to another and adopted two others. These children were:

Amelia Akoi, b. 1836, married Kamukai Victor, son of A'ina or CHEE In (徐燕).

Akana, b. circa 1839, child of Ahsam and Kamakahema.

Sam Kauehe, b. 1845, adopted, was son of Hapai and Iehu.

Harriet or Haliela, adopted, married Charles Kuinikinui (Akongee) Hapai.

Hapai, or LAU Fai (劉輝), arrived in the Islands around 1830. In 1838 he married Iehu, daughter of a high chief who had served on the council of Kamehameha the Great. The couple had eight children, one of whom, Sam Kauehe, was a hanai child to Aiko. Hanai was a common Hawaiian custom by which a child could be adopted informally by a relative or close friend.   Son Charles married Harriet, adopted daughter of Aiko.   Other children and their marriages were:

George Washington Akao, m. Harriet Rebecca K. Sniffen

Akananui, m. Charles Edward Richardson

Maikaaloa, m. Kahilo (?)

Ai Peter, m. Waiohinu

Akongee, aka Kuiniliilii, m. Sarah Kaina

Akanaliilii, m. Julius Lyman Richardson

Louisa, m. August Ahrens

The August Ahrens School in Waipahu, Oahu, is named after Louisa Hapai's husband.

Before arriving in Hilo, Hapai had been a partner with Aiko in a plantation at Iole.   In Hilo, he put up a sugar mill with John Ena, Sr., Akona, and Akau at the Ponohawaii Plantation.   In 1851 this plantation, consisting of 55 acres, produced 20,000 pounds of sugar.

Hapai died at the age of 83 in 1874 and was buried in Homelani Cemetery.

A'ina or CHEE In (徐燕) was in Hilo by 1835 and, with Akina or TANG Hung Sin (鄧行善), was sugar master for the well-liked Governor Kuakini of the Island of Hawaii.   A'ina was active in business and had property in Hilo as well as in Honolulu.   He first married Kaehe who died in 1846, and later he married Ana Kamakohema, previously mentioned.   The couple had a daughter, Maria, two sons, Mikaele and Vikoli Kamukai, who reversed and respelled his name to Kamukai Victor.   He did not use the so-called last name A'ina.   Kamukai Victor married Amelia Aiko, and they had eleven or twelve children; among them were A'ina Victor and Aiko Victor, named for their Chinese grandfathers.

There was also Keoniki Ko.   He may have been LAU Cheong (劉璋) who married Pukai.   They had one son Yan Kin who attended Mrs. Wetmore's School--a school strongly recommended by Hapai and an American businessman for children of the Chinese settlers and other children.   It was opened in 1850.

John Ena (ZANE), or TSENG Seong Hin (曾尚賢), was another sugar master.   Early Chinese were often called "John Chinaman."   The explanation of the Ena name can be traced to the Cantonese pronunciation of Hin which easily was Hawaiianized to Ena. John Ena, an active sugar planter at Ponohawaii, married Kaikilani, a chieftess, referred to as "Alii Wahine o Puna." Their daughter, Amoe Ululani, married High Chief Levi Haalelea. Another daughter, Laura Amoy, married John Coney. Ena Road in Waikiki is named after a son, John Ena, Jr.

Akau, or TANG Chow (鄧秋), may have been the brother of Akina. They had the same last name, TANG, which may also be pronounced Dung, Deng, or Dang. Akau and his wife Puanana, of Molokai of the <u>alii</u> (high ranking) class, had four sons: Charles who was married to Maria Iaukea, James to Amelia Higgins, William to Rose K. Stillman, and Akonoliilii Piehu to Emily K. Porter. This family belonged to St. Joseph Church.

This brings us to Akina, TANG Hung Sin (鄧行善), great-grandfather of Ernest Kai. Akina was in Hilo by 1840, as evidenced by a real estate transaction showing that he had acquired property in Piihonua that year. In 1851 his sugar plantation at Puueo was producing 100,000 pounds of sugar for export to Chinese stores in Honolulu. He also had in storage an additional 50,000 pounds of sugar and 3,900 gallons of molasses.

Akina's home was in Hilo at Piihonua, as were the homes of A'ina, Keoniki Ko, Aiko, Akau, and Hapai. Akina and his wife Kahilo had one son named John Kai Akina. John, in later years, dropped the Akina part of his name and became John Kai, explaining that Akina was not his father's real name. (Actually, if John wanted to use his father's real surname, he would have been John Kai TANG.)

Peggy Kai had married Ernest Kai, son of John Kai. She wrote a poignant story of <u>A'lai A'ii</u>, the Hawaiian-Chinese matriarch whose daughter, Annie Akamu, was the wife of John Kai and the mother of Ernest Kai. Peggy's delightful book contains many photographs and a comprehensive genealogy chart:

A'lai A'ii's father was TONG Yee (唐義); he was called A'ii. A'lai A'ii married LEONG Suk Kam (梁叔錦), called Akamu. Akamu took A'lai, their two daughters, and a son to China, where Akamu died. A'lai was very popular in the village. She had her sewing machine with her and helped her neighbors with their sewing. Also, A'lai was a beautiful, stately woman as were her three sisters. A Hawaiian song had been written about them, "Ka Pua o Kina." The girls were given Chinese names: A'ana, A'ima, A'lai, and A'oe.

As a widow, A'lai returned to Hilo with the girls, but left the son in China. A'lai later married WONG Kun (黄 根), called W. K. Akana. He was part of the next generation of Chinese in the Hilo community, as covered in a book which my husband, Tin-Yuke Char, and I wrote, <u>Chinese Historic Sites and Pioneer Families of the Island of Hawaii</u>.

[Margaret "Peggy" Hockley (Mrs. Ernest K.) Kai, died in January 1986. She was a member of the Hawaii Chinese History Center. Her research for her husband's Hawaiian-Chinese history sparked her enthusiastic interest in local Chinese history. My husband, Tin-Yuke, and I shared our knowledge of Chinese and our findings with her and feel privileged to have known her.]

CHINESE IN CENTRAL MAUI

Frederick Ten Soon Mau

I HAVE CHOSEN TO SPEAK briefly about the Chinese and part-Chinese and other people of the villages of Kamaole, Keokea, Koheo, and Ulupalakua, Maui.

Of the four goals mentioned in today's introductory speeches, I wish to call your attention to two: (1) to instill pride in and gratefulness for my part-Chinese heritage, and (2) to express appreciation for living in Hawaii and experiencing the joy of aloha.

I am grateful for my Chinese father, Mau Gim Biang. Born in 1870 in his ancestral village of Sun Chin, China, he came to Hawaii in 1894 at the age of 24. And for my mother who was born in the village of Kamaole in 1886. Her father was of Spanish descent and her mother was a full-blooded Hawaiian.

When he emigrated to Hawaii, my father was already married in China and had a son. After he married my mother and was established in Kamaole, he wanted his first wife and son to come to live here. She refused, because she may have felt that to come here, away from her homeland to live among strangers, would obligate her to "serve her in-laws."

My father operated the Hop Wo store in Kamaole, Maui. This store was first established by Chung Mook Heen, father of the former Chief Justice William H. Heen.

Besides being a general store, our Hop Wo store was a "mini community center." The Chinese farmers, especially those who were unable to read or write, depended on my father to write letters for them to their families and relatives in China, and to read to them the replies they received. Then there were the many cowboys, ranch hands, ranchers, and farmers who came to buy tailor-made work clothes of denim and khaki material and the famous checkered gingham material known as "palaka." My father served as tailor, as well as scribe and merchant.

Living in such an environment, as children of a storekeeper, we were especially blessed to have personal contact and association with people of different racial and cultural groups that lived in the community.

SPEAKING OF THE PEOPLE who lived in Kamaole and the neighboring villages of Keokea, Koheo, and Ulupalakua, I recall some of the Hawaiians with surnames, such as Kuhaulua, Hapakuka, Ha'ole, Kamakau, and Palai-le. Caucasians were Morton, Wallace, Thompson, Baldwin, MacFee, Tavares, DePonte, Ventura, Moniz, and Carvalho. Among the Chinese, the majority group, surnames, to mention a few, were Fong, Shim, Chong, Kong, Lee, Ching, Lau, Wong, Soon, Hew, Ing, Pang, Shinn, Luke, Tyau, Yap, Chun, and such Hawaiianized names as Akana, Akiona, Akuna, and Apo.

In the U.S. Census of 1910, I counted about 452 persons of Chinese and part-Chinese ancestry--men, women and children.

Of interest to me were the various occupations of the "head of family" listed in the Census report. I counted 80 "corn planters," farmers, and farm laborers, 8 merchants, 2 tailors, 2 druggists, 3 ministers, 6 clerks, 4 salesmen/peddlers, and 2 school teachers.

Living in a community of industrious people of various racial heritage and lineage, one learns to appreciate living in Hawaii and sharing the aloha spirit. From my Chinese father I learned about Chinese culture and traditions, and I developed a deep interest in learning more about my ancestry. Through my Spanish-Hawaiian mother I acquired the love of things Hawaiian--the culture, the traditions, and the aloha spirit.

The time allotted for my presentation today is shared with my sister-in-law, Bessie Tam-Loo Like. With her visual aids, tapestry, and photos, she will share her knowledge of Chinese families of Omaopio and Makawao.

In closing, I highly recommend that those interested in knowing more about the Chinese in Kula purchase the book by Diane Mei Lin Mark, published by the Hawaii Chinese History Center, entitled The Chinese in Kula: Recollections of a Farming Community in Old Hawaii.

My charts, photos, genealogical family group sheets and pedigree charts on the wall behind me, serve to emphasize the "catch word" of this conference, "Yum sai see yuen" -- "When drinking water, remember the source."

Thank you and aloha.

CHINESE OF KAUAI

Kam Hoon Young Lee

Kapaa

AFTER THE DEVASTATING KAPAA FIRE of 1923, our family had one of two remaining restaurants and bakeries. We became very busy. Lee Lin, the baker, made all the Chinese cakes. There were kong su biang, hung ngun biang, lat pee su, darn kau, tau sa bau, and ngau see biang. He also made the noodles using a bamboo stick about eight feet long and five or six inches across. First, he measured out the flour and made a hill of it on the pastry table, then he made a hole in the middle where he added the eggs and salt. He then mixed and kneaded the dough until it was elastic and didn't stick to his hands. The bamboo stick was used as a rolling pin, only he sat on it and jumped up and down to flatten the noodle dough. After awhile he would dust the dough with flour, fold it, and continue jumping up and down on the bamboo stick. He repeated this process until the dough was thin enough to cut into noodles and won ton wrappers. It looked like so much fun, very often I could not control my urge to jump on the bamboo stick when Lin turned his back. The baker did not appreciate my help and shooed me away. Raymond Chong Ching, a young man at the time, made all the pies and cakes. They both made the bread.

My father and mother did the rest of the cooking. We must have served very good food as the salesmen who came from Honolulu made it a point to arrive in Kapaa in time for lunch at our restaurant. Our steaks were freshly cut to each customer's order. The fresh mullet or akule, fried whole, rice, and vegetables were also popular items--a princely treat for fifty cents!

Our home was located in the heart of Kapaa town and this made it a very convenient stopping place for people to visit or to wait for family and friends. Mrs. Ching Kin Mui, who used to live in the Wailua Homesteads, often came to spend the day whenever she came to Kapaa. As we enjoyed her witty expressions, little did we realize that her grandson, Calvin Buck Hoy Ching, son of Dr. and Mrs. Edward Tim Ching, would someday marry my daughter, Wendy. Some of Mrs. Ching's other children were Ching Bun, Ching Fat, Ada Kwai Lee (Melvin) Lee, Ethel (Yan How) Lai, Ruth Lum, Harold Ching, and Constance Kwai Chun (Frederick) Chu.

One of my mother's favorite friends was Mrs. Ching Young of Hanalei. Their friendship started when Mrs. Ching Young came to Kapaa from Hanapepe as a bride. When she moved to Hanalei after her marriage, she used to stop over in Kapaa on her way to Lihue or Hanapepe. She often visited the Temple of the "Eight Immortals" (Bat Dai Sin) to consult with the immortals concerning business and family decisions. Thankful for the good advice received over the years, she would provide new outfits from Hong Kong to replace the worn-out ones for the "Eight Immortals" whenever needed. Her daughters, Dora and Laura, and I attended Kauai High School, and we enjoyed going to the many school functions together. We spent many weekends at each other's homes.

Another frequent visitor was Mrs. Gum Mung Shak whose husband was the manager of the Hawaiian Canneries in Kapaa. Mr. Shak loved to play golf. Their children were Lily Doong How (Norman) Au Hoy, a retired school teacher, Harold Karng You, Clarence Nam Sing, Arthur Ten Sing, Lawrence Wo Sing, and Allan On--all engineers.

When I went to Kauai High School, I rode with Gertrude Lin Jun and Reuben Tam in their car. Their parents were Mr. and Mrs. Tam Kee. My great-grandfather, Wong Aloiau, had married Mew Hin, sister of Tam Kee, who had accompanied her from China when she came for her marriage. Reuben, who has returned with his wife Gerry to live in Kapaa, was named one of seven outstanding artists in America by the American Academy and Institute of Arts and Letters in New York in 1978. His brothers and sister from the first mother are Dr. Henry Bung It of Texas, Harry Bung Hung, a retired banker of the American Security Bank, and Lin Ung (William) Ing, a retired school teacher.

After the death of his first wife, Tam Kee remarried, and the children from his second marriage are Marion Lin Hung (Arthur) Lynch, a retired dress designer; Gordon Bung Mung, proprietor of a sporting goods store in Kapaa; Priscilla Lin Kee (William) Leong, a retired school librarian in Kapaa; Phyllis Kam Ho (August) Yee, a community volunteer for drama and youth; Edwin Gung Lun, retired head of the Department of Public Welfare; Audrey Kam On (James) Chinn, a librarian at McKinley High School; and Harvey Bung Hau, a former photographer for the Garden Island Weekly.

Ching Sun Yau was our herbalist. He would feel our pulse whenever we were sick and prescribe the herbs for our cure. He sent for his wife and son, Wallace See Ng, from China. When Wallace graduated from Kauai High School, he and his family left Kauai to live in China, where he attended Lingnam University. Upon graduation, he returned to Hawaii and worked for the Pearl Harbor Navy Yard. His daughters are Frances and Bonnie.

Tom Lee, whose mother was Wong Aloiau's sister, was a partner in the Aloiau and Company rice plantation. Tom later ran a grocery store in Kapaa across the street from the Shido Store. When he moved his family to Honolulu in the 1920s, my father, Young Bong, and later my brother, Kwock Wai Young, took over Tom Lee's store, and renamed it Kapaa Mercantile Store and ran it until 1950. Tom Lee's children were sons Kwock Wo, Harry Kwock Sun, Robert Kwock Hin, Kwock Hoon, and Raymond Kwock Cheong, and daughter Winifred Sin Tau.

Chu Wai was the expert tailor of the town. His children were Wai Dung, Katherine Kai Mew, Lily, William Nam Hon, Kenneth, Theodore, and Barlow.

Mrs. Ching Kwong, a widow, lived with her sons, Koon Sung, Henry Koon Hin, Koon Wai, Charles, and daughter Bernice Sun Lee (Jack) Yee. Their cousins, children of Tom Kam Cheong, were Irene (Harry) Hee, Victoria (Harold) Wong, James, Richard, Warren, Nina, and Chester.

Wong Sam and his family ran Hop Wo Poi Shop, General Merchandise and Pork Butcher. His children from his first wife are Richard, Dr. Harry Yuen Chee, a cardiologist, Harriet Lin Pung Hayashi, and Harold Ah Lock. Hazel Kam Lin, Dorothy, and Howard Yee Kong are the issue from his second wife.

Fong Chong Sung, a merchant, had four sons—Kee Chong, Kee Fook, Henry Kee Look, and Kee Sau. His daughters were Gwendolyn and Cecilia.

There were eleven children in the Chu Inn family: Chun Moi (Francis) Loo, Frederick Fong Dong, an employee of the Hawaiian Telephone Company, Cecil Hung Kow, Catherine Chun Cook, Theresa Chun Ngit, Bernadette Kam Loi, Five Mee, a supervisor at the Wilcox Hospital, Harriet Chow Ngit, Lillian Chat Mui, Richard Lin Dung, and Sandra Bat Mui.

Wailua

Kai On (Kion) Soong, a former Wailua homesteader, was the best friend any child could have. During my fifth and sixth grade years, he would take my sister, my brothers, and me to visit the Cheong Hoon Wong family at the Wailua homestead. We enjoyed catching fish in the plantation ditches and playing with the children. The highlight of the visit was the delicious roasted capon chicken Mr. Wong himself raised and served. Two of his children, Gertrude Chung Oi (Walter) Pang and Minnie Ngan Hung (Herbert) Liu, were in Honolulu schools and came home only during vacations. At home were Vivian Choy Lan Eng, Stella Gum Pung (Koon Lee) Ching, Ruby Wei Hop Siu, Robert Mong Gun, Alvin Git Wong and Cyrus Say Loong.

Kai On Soong married Mary Ann Wong, daughter of Wong Hong Chung. The couple had two sons, Melvin Tin Yong Kaipoleimanu, who was an assistant to U.S. Attorney Walter Heen in Honolulu and is now a judge in the courts, and Clarence Launane, who is in Japan and employed by the U.S. government there; and a daughter, Momelani Sum Tai, a school teacher, is married to Cmdr. Julian Kau of the U.S. Navy. Mr. Soong was employed by the Chinese American Bank, renamed American Security Bank, and later at the County Tax Office. He retired as the director of the Civil Service Commission of Kauai County. Mary Ann retired from the Labor Department and later served as librarian of Hawaiiana at the Coco Palms Resort in Wailua. After retirement, the couple served as missionaries in Hong Kong for the Mormon Church.

There were many luaus at the homestead, but I especially remember the extra delicious food at the home of Tai Yung Lum, also known as Lum Yung. Those old-fashioned luaus were replete with kalua pig, raw fish, and opihis. The Lums had a big family: Clemens Kam Hoon, Molly Kam Sai (Gilbert) Williams, Eva Kam Yee (Arthur) Shak, Harriet Kam How (Frank) Meid, Annie Kam Oi (Harry) Conching, Benjamin Kam Sung, Christina Kam Moi Ikeda, Lydia Woon Sinn (Lawrence) Au, Ada Kwai Lee (Ronald) Conching, Elizabeth Kam Hung (George) Takahashi, Francine Kam Lin (Robert) Castro, Joseph, Lloyd Chu Leong, Raymond Sun Yet, and Daniel Chu Kin.

The Bung Yung Apana family lived in the coconut grove which is now the Coco Palms Hotel. Their children are Ah Chin, Ah Bau, Ah Chan, Alice Aiu, Ah Choy, and Helen.

Kealia

Chong Ah Hoon was the head sugar boiler for the Makee Sugar Plantation in Kealia, where he and his family lived. His children were Kam Fong Hee, Emily Kam Chung Kaohu, Nellie Yau Yee Shim, Wai Yen, Edna Kam Lan, and Albert Wai Foon.

Yong Hum started as a cook's assistant at Aloiau's rice plantation. Later he was a sugar cane contractor for the Makee Plantation which provided him with several acres of land to plant sugar cane. His income was dependent on what he harvested every eighteen months. The Yong family left for Honolulu in 1925. The children were Irene Tung Lin (David) Au, Harry Ah Tong, Patsy Yau Kum Georgette, Myrtle Yau Hoon, Kwai Chong, Kwai Wah, Lydia Yau Chun Len, and Thelma Yau Sin (Albert) Chun.

In the Lui Oi family were Dr. Alfred Lui, Stanford, Dr. Percy Lui, and their sister Marjorie.

Another Kealia family was the Liu Mung household: Herbert Wing Kwai, a retired Farrington High School teacher, Mabel Mee Que Wong, Albert, Beatrice Kam How Bortner, Sunny Wing Chun, and David Wing Sam.

Chong Fook Yee had a bakery and restaurant in Kealia. Among his children were Gladys, Herman, Elsie, Albert, and Mary Jane.

Anahola

Mrs. Lai Tom Shee and her family were rice planters in Anahola. She had four sons: (1) Lai Yun Chung, whose sons were Edwin Jun Him Lai, chief field tax auditor for the State, Wallace Jun Duk Lai, president and manager of Mid Pacific Lumber, and Dr. Leonard Lai, an orthodontist; (2) Lai Yan Tim, who was employed at Garden Island Motors, and whose wife Carlotta was the principal of Anahola School; (3) Lai Yan How, proprietor of Kapaa Meat Market, is the father of Koon Kin and Koon Chau, who supply the Islands with their well-known kulolo and poi; (4) Lai Yan Yin worked for his brother, Yan How, in running the meat market.

Also in Anahola was the Ching Kau family. They were Raymond Chong Ching, Anna Choy Sung Tom, Bernice Choy Hu Hee, Kenneth Yu Hung Ching, a chef in a Kona hotel, Florence Choy Lee Boren, and Vivian Choy Hop Lewis. Anna married Yau Sung Tom and lived in Kapaa. Their children are Douglas K. W. Tom, who is with the National Guard in Hilo, George Q. W. Tom, National Guard in Honolulu, and Roy E. W. Tom, a specialist in instrument making for the University of Hawaii. Bernice married Hee Dai Chong. Their son Roger Hee is a former councilman for Kauai County.

Kapaia

In Kapaia the Ching Din family members were Koon Wing, Larry Koon Wai, Shew Young Leong, Koon Yee, Oi Kam, Koon Chee, and Mew Lung.

The other Chinese family in Kapaia belonged to Fong Dai Kum, who had a rice mill and store. The sons were Ah Chock, Robert, Dr. Koon Sut Fong, and Koon Yin, Ah Chock's children were Roland Quon Hin, Kenneth Quon Shew, Allen Q. L., Donald Q. N., Marian (Stanley) Au, Diana (Sau Yet) Lum, Gladys (Stanley Kim) Lau, and Eleanor (Melvin O. Q.) Dang.

Lihue

The Chun Lin Hung family of Lihue, better known as the Ahanas, produced two strong politicians. Koon Cheong and Koon Mung Ahana were county auditor and treasurer, respectively, for many years. There were also Ah Sau and Ah Wo Ahana and their sister, Harriet Ahana Albao.

Hanapepe

Hee Hong opened a Chinese restaurant and bakery in Hanapepe. His children are Wah Sun, Wah Ching, Harry Wah Ming, Wah Kin, and Mollie Ching of Kapaa.

Ah Yet Dang, a brother of Mrs. Ching Young, also lived in Hanapepe. His sons were Wah Git, Wah Fai, and Wah Yun, and his daughters were Lo Sun (Tai Hing) Leong, Ah Kam (James) Wong, and Ah Hoon Dang.

Waimea

Shui Sang Ching, a rice grower in Waimea, had three sons and four daughters. They were Sarah Look Moi (Reuben) Chang, Ah Fook, Edward You Choi, Dr. Gilbert Ching, a doctor at Leahi Hospital, Alice Ah Tai (Joseph) Aiu, Grace Ah Keau (Vernon) Yap, and Clara Sum Oi (Gregory) Ho.

Another family from Waimea was the Hee Hong See family. Their son, Hong Shin, was a comptroller, and son, Hong Min, a field overseer of the Kekaha Sugar Plantation. Gilbert is with American Factors in Honolulu; Roberta Sau Lin (Fred) Dang is in charge of personnel at Woolworth at Waialae-Kahala; Mew Sin Lee lives in Boston; and Mew Lun Wong, in Orange County, California.

Mr. Ching Ako (Kin Sai) ran a general store in Waimea. He later left for Honolulu, and his son Chung Mee Ako took over the business. Kin Sai's first wife bore him three sons. The oldest son, Ah Yew, left to live in China. The second son, Kwan Chew Ching, lived at Port Allen with his wife and daughters, Lorraine (Hon Chong) Chang and Florence (Allan) Richardson, and son, Richard. The third son, Hung Wan Ako, had three sons and three daughters: Francis, a real estate broker, Lawrence, a retired counselor from the Honolulu Community College, Harry, May, Katherine, and Kathleen Ako. The following are the children from Ching Ako's (Kin Sai) second marriage: Beatrice Yuk Hoong, Chung Mee, Rose Yuk Ung Au, Alice Yuk Jun Yee, Edith Kwock Hung Chang, Bessie Kam Hung Furukawa, Lily Lai Kin Wong, Esther Yuk Inn Ahuna, Gardie Yuk Oi Chock, and Myrtle Yuk Ngun Kung.

Hanalei, Kalihiwai, and Kilauea

Ching Young sold his share of the Kapaa store and restaurant, Kwong

Chong Kee, to Tam Kee around 1914, and moved to Hanalei. In his new location, he opened the Ching Young Store and Ching Young Rice Mill. After Ching Young died in 1933, Mrs. Ching took over the management of the businesses and educated the children. They were Florence Mew Sun Ching, Dora Mew Gau (Edward) Murashige, Laura Ah Wah (Howard) Lum, Lawrence Lin Tai, present proprietor of the Ching Young Shopping Center in Hanalei, Douglas Lin Pung, an engineer in California, Calvin Lin Keong, an engineer with his own firm on Kauai, and Janet Mew Jun Webster, living in California.

Also in Hanalei lived the children of the Chock Chin family. They were Nee Chang (Harry) Wong, Ardith (Joseph) Lam, Harry, Janet Pearl, and Hugh Chock. According to Nee Chang Chock Wong, Chock Chin's store, which also included a coffee shop and bakery, was already doing business in Hanalei by 1901 as C. Akeoni. He was already in the baking business by 1898 and had a rice plantation by 1901, which produced $5,000 worth of business. The plantation was located in Waikoko and was leased from G. N. and Sam Wilcox.

The Ho Sau Hin family included Kan Sing, Harry, a retired school principal of Haena, Koolau, and Anahola Schools, Annie Miller, Joyce Fountain, Florence Ching, and Clarabelle.

Other Hanalei families were Tom Low, Ching Ma Leong, Wong Duck, Say Duck, Lum Dat, Kam Hee, and Wong Lee Yau.

Albert Goo of Kalihiwai was a fisherman. He is the son of Goo Bark Tai. His sisters are Fanny, a public school teacher, and Caroline Albao.

K. C. Lung, the owner of the Kilauea Plantation Store, developed his site into a modern shopping center.

[Editor's note: In addition to Kam Hoon Y. Lee's presentation at the Conference, this paper includes unusual genealogical information from her unpublished paper of 1979 on the Chinese of Kauai.]

CHINESE IN KAHALUU AND KANEOHE

Henry C. F. Lau

MY RESPONSIBILITY TODAY is to tell you about the Chinese in the Waikane through the Kaneohe areas. Between the years 1870 and 1925, there were acres and acres of rice fields and nine to ten rice mills in the area. Pineapples were grown in Heeia, Ahuimanu, and Kahaluu, and the first Libby cannery was located in Kahaluu. With rice and pineapples beginning to fade out in 1925, most of the Chinese families moved to other parts of the Island. Today, small-scale farming still exists in the Kahaluu and Waikane areas, but Kahaluu has gone urban the past fifteen to twenty years and now has an estimated population of over 10,000. Kahaluu is going to be a big town in the very near future.

I'll be mentioning the names of Chinese families that I know lived in the area and hope that at least one of those families mentioned may be of some interest to you. It could be a family with your family name or surname. If it is, I hope you will be interested enough to work further on your Chinese roots by contacting that family to see whether they have their family genealogy to share with you and to see how or whether you are related. (I can furnish most of their addresses.) Remember one thing: working on your genealogy is not an overnight matter; it is time-consuming and continuing, and you must have patience. It is very challenging and also can be very rewarding.

Now, for the families that lived in the Waikane and Kaneohe areas:

Lau, Hin Young. I would like to start off with my father Lau Hin Young, better known as Lau Kau. He emigrated from China in 1890 when he was 15 years old. He is from Kwangtung province, Chung Shan, Leong Doo, Buck Toy village. He settled in the Kaalaea-Kahaluu area and was first employed as a kitchen helper at the Kaalaea Rice Mill. He had other chores, too, like planting rice and growing vegetables. He started a small grocery store in 1910, and at the same time owned and managed his own rice fields for many years. I can still remember those years in the late 1920s. Each day after school and every Saturday and Sunday we were down in the rice fields chasing birds or doing other chores on the farm. We never had any time for recreation. It was work, work, work. I cherish those hard experiences. I must thank my father for his foresight and the hardship he went through to make things so much easier for us in our generation. My dad was a very generous man. He always helped other families in trouble and never asked for anything in return.

Back in 1906, he had returned to China to marry a young girl from Hang Mee village, by the name of Lee Look. That was his last trip back to China. He wanted to visit the village later, but could not make it because the communists were in control. In 1956 he made it only to Hong Kong and Macau.

Our record of the Lau family shows the direct line of our forefathers way back to the 1100s. The chart is from the first generation Lau from the Chung Shan district to the 26th generation. I keep a record of my brothers' and sisters' families also and update these records whenever there is a marriage, birth, or death. If you are a Lau and need some help in your genealogy, I can help you. Or, if you know of any Lau who is interested in genealogy, let him know and have him contact me.

Now, for the other families who lived in the area. [Unless otherwise stated, all families were from Kwangtung province, Chung Shan district.]

Ching, Gam Cheong. He left China in 1888 for Hawaii, is from See Dai Doo, Nam Long. He settled in the Waiahole-Waikane area for about 15 years as a rice farmer, but moved to Punaluu in the early 1900s. One of his sons, Quan Yen Ching, is a retired government worker living in Honolulu.

Au, Dai Sau. He left China about 1875 to come to Hawaii and is also from See Dai Doo, Nam Long. He settled in Waikane as a rice farmer. His son is Au, Goon Wah. His grandson, Henry Tuck Au, is an engineer in Honolulu.

Young, Mun Luke. In 1890 he left China for Hawaii and settled in Waikane for 20 years as a rice farmer and then moved to Wahiawa. He is from Gook Doo, Ook Sak. He had six sons and four daughters. One of his sons Lum Chow Young lives in Honolulu.

Wong, Yau. He left China in 1895 for Hawaii. He is from See Dai Doo, Seu Yin village. He was a rice farmer and settled in Waikane. One of his sons is William T.S. Wong, who lives in Honolulu.

Thom, Huen. About 1890 he left China and went directly to California. Later he came from there to settle in Waikane where he lived for 33 years. He was the owner-operator of Waikane Store which is still there. His sons all live on Oahu. Among them is Erwin Wah Chu Thom, who is now retired and has passed on his businesses to his children. He was the owner-manager of Foremost Finance, had the franchise for Dairy Queen and had a sporting goods store.

Lee, Lum Sau. A native of Loong Doo district, Sarn Chin village, he left China in 1875. He settled in Waikane where he lived for 30 years and was the manager of the rice mill there. His sons are Kam Tai and Reuben. Kam Tai Lee was the treasurer of the Territory of Hawaii at one time.

Chang, Hee. He left China about 1889 from Gook Doo district, Sarm Heung village. He settled in Waikane, was a rice farmer, and had four boys and three girls. One of the sons is Kenneth K.C. Chang of Honolulu.

Kong, Lee Sun. In the late 1890s he left China and settled in the Heeia area before moving to Waikane. He was a rice farmer; had two boys and three girls. Henry Kong, in his early 80s, is the only living child and still lives in Waikane.

Chun, Marn Sung. He left China from See Dai Doo district, Cha Inn village. He settled in Waihole and was occupied in many businesses besides being a rice farmer. He had eight boys. Two sons, Henry Hyok Han Chun and John Chun, were my classmates in Waihole School in the late 1920s.

Lau, Yen Dai. He left China in the late 1890s from Leong Doo district, Buck Toy village, and settled in Kaalaea. He was a rice farmer for a short while, then moved to Honolulu to open up a grocery store on Pauahi Street. He had three sons and two daughters who are all living in Honolulu.

Tom, How Choy. In 1890 he left from Leong Doo district, Buck Toy village, China. He was a rice farmer and settled in Kahaluu; had one son and two daughters.

Loo, Pung. He left China in 1885 from Goong Sheong Doo district, Bark San village. He was the manager of the rice mill in Kaalaea, and had two sons and one daughter. One of his sons is Loo Chow who still has children living in the Kahaluu and Kaneohe areas.

Wong, Dau. He left China in the late 1890s from Leong Doo district, Loong Tong village. He operated and managed the Kahaluu Fish Pond. Being a generous and kind man, he would let us kids catch crabs and fish in his pond. He has one son, Chew Leong Wong, presently the executive secretary for the United Chinese Society.

Yim, Lun Chee. He came to Hawaii in 1900 from See Dai Doo district, Nam Long village. He farmed for awhile then operated a grocery store in Kaneohe where he owned several business properties now managed by his children. He had five boys and a girl. The three older boys, Walter, Clarence, and Herbert, are now retired. Evans is semi-retired from his real estate business and Henry, the youngest, is a doctor in Kaneohe.

Chang, Lum Kin. He left China in 1880 when he was only 18 years old. He started as a rice farmer and later owned and operated a store in Heeia and also operated his own rice mill and rice fields. He had four boys and four girls.

Lu, Hung. He left Goong Sheong Doo district, Ha Chak village, China in 1879 and became a rice farmer. He married Yee, Gun Loong from See Dai Doo district, Nam Long village. They had six sons and three daughters.

Yim, Hoon Wai. In 1890 he came to Hawaii from See Dai Doo district and settled in Kaneohe. He raised and butchered pigs for a living, selling his pork to farmers from Kailua to Kahaluu. He has a son who lives in Canada and two daughters who still live in Kaneohe.

There are other families who lived in the Kahaluu area for whom I have little or no information. There is a Leonard Wong family who moved into Kaalaea from Moanalua in the 1950s. He is successfully growing taro tops (luau leaves).

Others who lived in the area are the Wong Tong family, Lum Chan family, Liu family, Ching family, and Choy family.

I would like to pass on some important steps I took in completing the genealogy of my family:

1. Find out the province, district, and village of your father or grandfather who came from China.

2. Find persons with the same surname from the same village and ask them whether they have their family genealogy.

3. Ask others with the same surname for their genealogy. Usually, those with the same surname would have some family ties. For instance, I'm a Lau, and I can help those persons with a Lau surname.

4. Ask members of your "Surname Chinese Society" and "District Chinese Society" to help.

5. Contact family members in China to help with your family genealogy.

It took me seven years to complete my genealogy, from 1976 through 1983, and I took two trips to China to my father's village to get some family records. Just recently on TV, a Ching family from Hawaii said that it took them ten years to complete theirs. Genealogy researching is not an overnight matter, it is continuing, and you must keep at it.

I wish all of you the best of luck in seeking out your Chinese roots. Thank you.

CHINESE OF PUNALUU

Wah Chan Ching

GOOD AFTERNOON! My name is Wah Chan Ching, a third-generation resident of Hawaii, born and raised in Punaluu.

In talking story with you about the Chinese of Punaluu today, we hope that we can impart some information supplemental to your reading of James H. Chun's book, The Early Chinese in Punaluu, hereafter referred to as the "book." The figures in parenthesis indicated herein represent the page numbers of the book.

For those of you who are inclined to find your Punaluu roots after today's session, we hope that our discussion will help to facilitate your efforts.

As you may be aware, most of the early Chinese pioneer residents of Punaluu originally came to Hawaii from the Nam Long area of See Dai Doo, Chungshan, in Kwangtung province.

The Nam Long area is situated midway between Shekki, capital of Chungshan County (now Zhongshan City), and Choy Hang (now Tsuihang), the birthplace of Dr. Sun Yat-sen. The early Chinese of Punaluu came from villages in Nam Long such as Cha In, Cho Bu Tau, Hahng Mee, Nam Long Hee, On Dang, Tin Bin, Lai Chin, Sai Chien, Tai Leang Tau, Sai Hang, etc.

James Chun states in his book,

> "Between the latter part of the nineteenth century and the early years of the twentieth, this fertile plain from Kaaawa to Hauula was settled by hard-working people from China.
>
> "For our purpose we will call this strip of land lying between the foothill of the Koolau Mountains and the shoreline of the Pacific Ocean, Punaluu. This includes the entire plain from Kaaawa to Hauula.
>
> "The names of these places--Kaaawa, Kahana, Punaluu, Kaluanui, and Hauula--are Hawaiian, but the culture--speech, religion, politics, festivals, and outlook--was Chinese." (2)

In our discussion today, we will endeavor to help you find the approximate location where the various Punaluu families lived, in relation to the landmarks mentioned in the book. We hope that you will help to correct any errors or omissions on our part.

Kaaawa

Beginning with Kaaawa and proceeding toward Hauula, we start with the home of Yuen Kang Mui. It was located approximately 500 yards from, and on the Honolulu side of, Kaaawa Elementary School, and about 100 yards mauka of Kamehameha Highway. The Yuens were peanut farmers.

Kahana

Traveling past Kaaawa Beach Park and the Crouching Lion Inn, we approach Kahana Bay. After crossing the bridge at Kahana Stream, we reach Kahana Beach Park located on the makai side of the highway. Directly opposite is Kahana State Park. The adjacent road leads into Kahana Valley. Here, about 200 yards inland from the highway, lived the families of Chang Joy and Kam Mung. The Changs operated a bakery and the Kams, a country store.

Punaluu

After Kahana, we come to Punaluu where the majority of the Chinese families resided. The following families lived in the area about half a mile beyond Kahana Beach Park and Punaluu Beach Park: Ching Hoy, Ching Hin Tai, Yuen Pui Dip, Yuen Hong Kwai, Lum Ngin Soong, Yuen Pui Geang, Yuen Pui Ngew, and Chung Wai Yum.

Choy Hong Lai lived along Punaluu Valley Road which began at a point opposite the Honolulu end of Punaluu Beach Park. About a mile inland from the highway is the spot where the annual Ching Ming Memorial Service is held (37). My father, who was born in 1892, has been coming to this spot annually since he was a youngster. The Wong Kwai Rice Mill--generated by water power--was located nearby.

Just past Punaluu Beach Park is Waiono Stream. Crossing the bridge, we come to the home of Chun Man Chu, where James H. Chun was born.

At the site of the present Ching Punaluu Store, lived the family of Ching Wai Fong (66). My father, Ching Yan Quong, who is 93 years old, was born and still resides at this location.

The Green Valley Road leads to the jungle training camp where the army trained during World War II. The homes of Ching Kan You (79) and Hee Chong were reached through this road.

Back along Kamehameha Highway is the Doong Chong Store (36, 69). Built in 1906, it "stands today as the only man-made landmark of an age gone by." It was owned and operated by the Seu Tin Ung (Aana) family. Subsequently, it was operated by Tong Hong, a widower with five sons, who moved to Punaluu from Waikane prior to 1920.

Nearby neighbors were the families of Ching Wai Wai, Chun Hoon (Ahuna), Ching Hin Kong, and Ching Shai.

The Yin Sit Sha clubhouse (44), erected in 1907, was situated at the site where two duplex units now stand (47). The income derived from this property enabled the society to sponsor the publication of The Early Chinese in Punaluu.

99

Near the clubhouse were the homes of Lum Ngin Garm, Ching Wong Kee, Lee Lun, Chang Choy, and Ching Leong. Up towards the hillside on Haleaha Road lived Au Hee, Leong Wah See, and Ching Song.

Further along Kamehameha Highway, near the present Kaya Store, were the families of Au Kin (brother of Au Hee), who operated a bakery, and Leong Wah Tung (brother of Leong Wah See). The Chinese Protestant Church (29) and the Catholic Church (30) near Pat's at Punaluu, were located in the vicinity.

Kaluanui

The families in Kaluanui were Wong Chan, Wong Sung Chew (81), Goo Yoong Duck, Char Boon (the only Hakka family in Punaluu), Ching Tin Sung, and Ching Ung Chong.

The Lin Hop Rice Mill (16) was located next to the first Ching Tong Sing (son of Ching Ung Chong) Store (92).

Hauula

In the vicinity of Hauula Elementary School lived the families of Chun Hin (Ahina), Ching Tong Leong, Ing Koon Sum, and Ing Koon Ting.

The Ching Tong Leong Store (38) is the site where the roast pig was chopped up after the annual Ching Ming Memorial Service. The store is now operated by Lawrence K.L. Ching, son of Ching Tong Leong.

Reaching Punaluu

To reach Punaluu by public transportation, take TheBus on Route 55 via Circle Island/Kaneohe or Circle Island/Wahiawa.

Additionally, to locate rural area addresses, refer to the home address or telephone post number in order to narrow your search.

In closing, we thank you for your kind attention.

- Prepared by <u>Wah Chan Ching</u> for the Conference, "Researching One's Chinese Roots," Saturday, July 27, 1985, McKinley High School

for the Hawaii Chinese History Center
   111 North King St., Room 410
   Honolulu, HI 96817

Island of Oahu

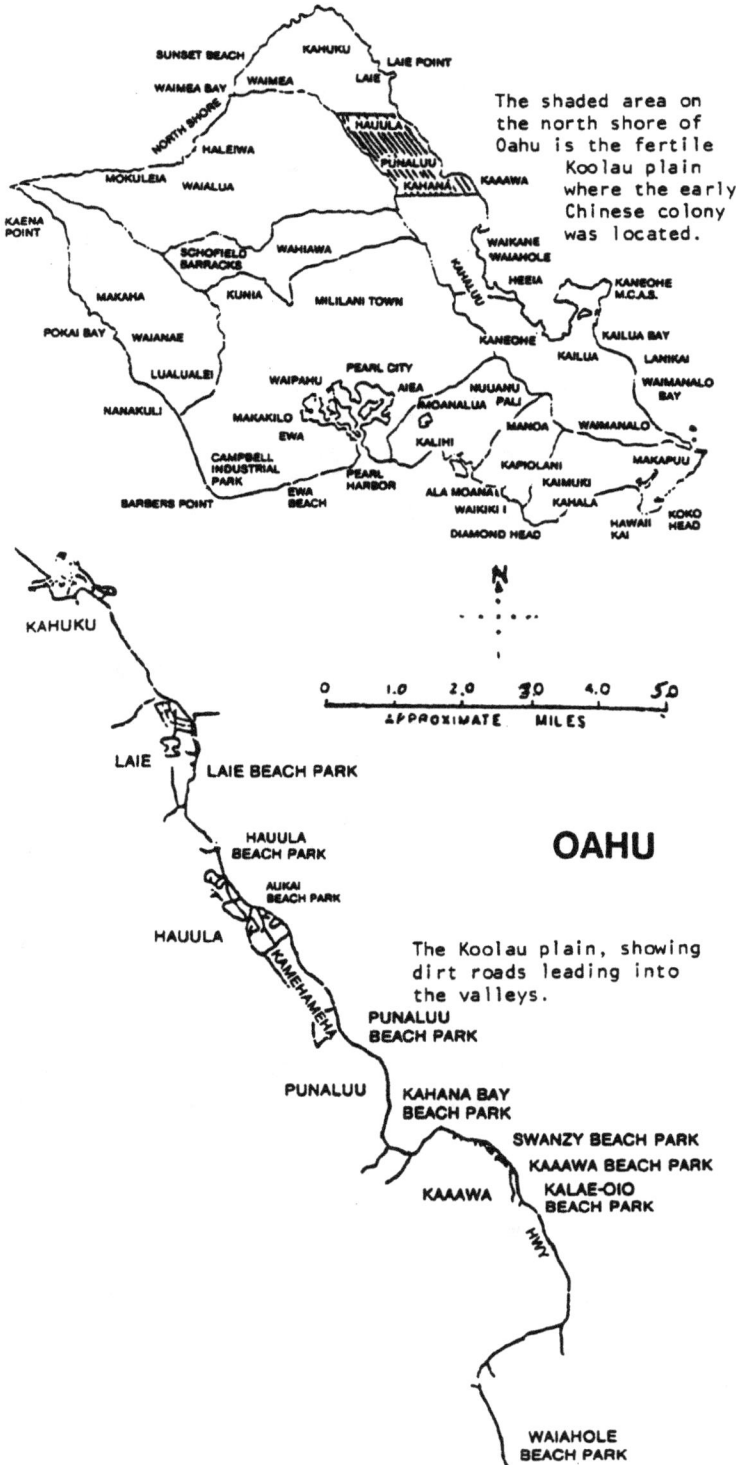

The shaded area on the north shore of Oahu is the fertile Koolau plain where the early Chinese colony was located.

The Koolau plain, showing dirt roads leading into the valleys.

Ancestral Village:

A. Cha In
B. Cho Bu Tau
C. Hahng Mee
D. Nam Long Hee
E. Ong Dang
F. Lai Chin
G. Sai Chien
H. Tai Leang Tau
I. Tong Kar Heong
J. Sai Hang

Chinese of Punaluu

Kaaawa
1. Yuen, Kang Mui
Kahana
2. Chang, Joy
3. Kam, Mung
Punaluu
4. Ching, Hoy
5. Ching, Hin Tai
6. Yuen, Pui Dip
7. Yuen, Hong Kwai
8. Lum, Ngin Soong
9. Yuen, Pui Giang
10. Yuen, Pui Ngew
11. Choy, Hong Lai
12. Chun, Man Chu
13. Ching, Wai Fong
14. Ching, Gan You
15. Ching, Wai Wai
16. Ching, Hin Kong
17. Ching, Shai
18. Seu, Tin Aana
19. Tong, Hong
20. Chun, Hoon (Ahuna)
21. Lum, Ngim Garm
22. Ching, Kwong Kee
23. Lee, Lun
24. Chang, Choy
25. Ching, Leong
26. Ching, Wai Yum
27. Au, Hee
28. Hee, Chong
29. Au, Kin
30. Leong, Tung
31. Leong, See
32. Ching, Song
Kaluanui
33. Wong, Sing Chew
34. Goo, Yoong Duck/Wong, Chan
35. Char, Boon
36. Ching, Tin Sung
37. Ching, Ung Chong
Hauula
38. Chun, Hin (Ahina)
39. Ching, Tong Leong
40. Ing, Koon Sum
41. Ing, Koon Ting

Taken from

THE EARLY CHINESE IN PUNALUU

by

James H. Chun

CHINESE IN TIN CAN ALLEY

Helen Hu Wong

"TIN CAN ALLEY," as it was known in the late 1930s through the World War II years, was officially named Kamanuwai Lane. It was a short and narrow lane, full of holes, sloping down from Beretania Street to the small Nuuanu Stream which emptied into the ocean near River Street.

As a youngster, I used that lane as a shortcut from my home on River Street to go to Chinatown or to Beretania Mission. I remember especially the family-run stores and the residential apartment buildings crowded on both sides of the lane. The people living there were respectable persons of Hawaiian, Chinese, and Japanese ancestry. Perhaps there were other ethnic groups represented, but I do not recall any.

How this lane became known as "Tin Can Alley" I didn't know until much later. I was told that, with the change of inhabitants, the place deteriorated and became a dumping ground for empty tin cans. The galvanized iron theater, a former favorite which showed exciting cowboy and travel movies, had been converted to unveil burlesque shows, accompanied by "tinny" sounding music every night. These shows attracted the many single military men and other transients.

But now, I'd like to reminisce about the better days of "Tin Can Alley." Lai Say, a "Tin Can Alley" resident, arrived from China aboard the Siberian in 1870. He and a relative organized the Hop Sing Store located on Hotel Street. The store sold imported items from China. Lai was the founder of the How Wong Miu Temple, which embraced a combination of Taoism, Buddhism, and Confucianism. A two-story structure located on 10,000 square feet of land behind an apartment building, housed the temple on the second floor and Lai's family on the first floor. He and his wife had six boys and four girls. One son, Lai Tin, became a well-known baseball player. All the children grew to be upright citizens, and in 1985 the three survivors are Mrs. Annie Sunn, mother of Franklin Sunn, Lee Lai, and Mrs. Jessie Young, a dear friend of mine from early days. She provided the photograph for this article and also the information on her family and the How Wong Miu.

After Lai Say's death, Mrs. Lai took over the custodial duties plus helped the followers observe temple rites and build their faith in the temple's patron god.

The temple later caught fire, but was rebuilt. Religious activities continued until the City and County of Honolulu started the redevelopment project. Inhabitants of "Tin Can Alley" were all evicted. The How Wong Miu was then moved to Liliha Street to the present site of St. Theresa Church. After the death of Mrs. Lai Say in her 90s, the temple made two additional moves, the last to Lum Say Ho Tong.

Another impressive two-story structure was the Kwong Yi Tong Society Building for restaurant owners and their employees. The assembly hall was located on the second floor, complete with kitchen and bathrooms. Nearby was the apartment for the Chinese custodian whose Hawaiian in-laws and their friends frequently came to socialize and create much havoc after their alcoholic consumption.

Apartments for families, which were mostly Chinese, were located downstairs. Community kitchens, toilets, and bathrooms were installed in the back, adjacent to our yard.

Another landmark was the Jook Pu, a small flourishing restaurant with shelves placed along the walls to serve as tables. Serving as cook and waiter, Lee Buck Yuen, the aged proprietor, prepared "kup dai jook," a favorite rice soup featuring chopped pork dumplings, pig liver, and pig intestines. The rich stock was made from pig jaw bones, complete with the molars intact. Many a poor family benefited from the generosity of Lee when he doled out his unsold soup late in the evening.

CHINESE IN WAIALUA AND HALEIWA

Jacob Ng

Introduction

This report of the Chinese of Waialua includes Haleiwa, and covers the area from Kaena Point to Waimea Bay on the north shore, in the years 1920 to 1945. Due to financial reasons, the area declined after World War II.

Haleiwa was the major center for the Chinese whose social and cultural life revolved around the many stores, a Chinese society, and a temple located at Waialua Beach Road and Weed Junction. The population, about 200, consisted of many single males who were employed by the sugar plantation. Farming and store keeping were other main sources of employment.

Stores as Centers

Organized in the 1920s were Yee Hop Market, Achiu Brothers, and Ah Leong Store. In 1930 came Jan Hing Store and Lau Kong Store; in 1935, Ng Fong Store, and in 1946, Chun's Store. The original owners of Yee Hop Market were Chun Tim, who died at 94, and Wong Chung, who returned to China for health reasons and died there. Chun Tim sold his interests for $1,000 to Wong Chung and later to Ng Fong.

Tai Sing Society

The Tai Sing Society was located in Haleiwa, near Weed Junction. Its purpose was to maintain a cemetery for the Chinese and to perpetuate their custom of observing Ching Ming or Hung Ting annually. This cemetery consisted of a central grave to honor the first person buried there, namely, Ah Goong San, and several other individual graves.

Chinese Presently Living in Waialua

Still active are two very senior citizens--Mrs. Chun Tim at 92 and Mrs. Ng Fong at 86. Others are Andrew Liu and family, Harry Ung and his sister Annie, John Chun and family, Jacob Ng and family, and State Representative Joseph Leong and family.

The Ng Family

Ng Fong, the patriarch, arrived from Kwangtung, Toi Shan, See Yup Village in 1894 at age 22. He was contracted to work on Maui and the Big Island at $10.00 a month. When he left for Honolulu to work, he had no money; a loaf of bread had to last him for two days. He worked at Kahuku Sugar Company and later he moved to Waialua and started business as a door-to-door vendor. In 1935 he opened the Ng Fong Store in Waialua near the Long Bridge. His available asset was $600 which was supplemented by his wife's jewelry. His store served the community for 25 years and closed in 1960.

Mrs. Ng Fong is now 86 years old. She came from Kwangtung Province, Toi Shan of See Yup Village in 1922. Her trip took one month by ship.

Yesteryears

Campbell Farm, located in Mokuleia, hired Chinese farm hands.

Mokuleia Rice Mill, owned and operated by Wong Mun See, husked all the rice grown in Haleiwa.

Leong Dai Chi operated the grocery store located at the present site of the Chevron Station in Waialua.

Jan Hing Store, managed by the Yuen family, was a grocery and general merchandise store. Today, houses occupy the former site of the store.

"Froggy" (Mr. Lai?), a kung fu expert, was a frog farmer and poolroom operator.

Tim Fung and Tim Hop Achiu were ranchers in Waialua.

Achiu Brothers Store was the first Chinese store in the 1920s on the sugar plantation. It was located across the street from the Otake Store in Waialua. The early store had no modern refrigeration and depended on ice blocks. It was distinguished by a large sign of Chinese calligraphy on a red background. Mrs. Achiu had small bound feet. The children were Tin Fun, Tin Hop, and Walter Achiu, a famous Chinese wrestler.

Henry Ching was an important commercial fisherman who specialized in akule. Lau Kong Store, a landmark, was located near the Long Bridge in Waialua. The Yee family was a large one with three boys and six girls.

Chun Kwan Chong, who came from Chung Shan, China, lived until he was 92. He worked for the Hakalau Plantation on the Big Island and was a fish peddler in Honolulu before he went to Waialua to work at the sugar plantation, Waialua Agricultural Company, in 1922. As a rice farmer in 1924, he leased land from James Awai. Chun also grew lotus root (lin ngow). In 1946 his son John Chun and John's wife Rachel started the John/Rachel Chun Store, a pioneer mini shopping center in Waialua.

Chun Tim, an old pioneer in Haleiwa, has a family composing of Henry, Herbert, Ah Lung, Leila, and Ah Howe.

The Plantation

Jim Wong, now deceased, was the mill foreman at the Waialua Agricultural Company where he was employed for over 40 years. He and his wife, Violet, were well-known for having planted the algaroba tree fronting the Waialua Public Library. Fook Chin Liu, retired, worked as a boilerman for the same company.

CHINESE OF UPPER FORT STREET

Hung Sum Nip and Theodore H. K. Tom

GOOD AFTERNOON, EVERYONE. I'd like to welcome all of you to this session where we will discuss the many Chinese families residing in this so-called Fort Street area. Since both Theodore H.K. Tom and I were born and raised in this sector, we are familiar with most of the Chinese families. Mr. Tom is very prominent in the local Chinese community. He is the immediate past president of the See Dai Doo Society, one of the largest Chinese societies in the Islands, a graduate of Mun Lun Chinese School, member of Chee Kung Tong, and also a teacher of ballroom dancing. My name is Hung Sum Nip, also a graduate of Mun Lun Chinese School. Presently I'm a trustee for the United Chinese Society, emeritus director for the Chinese Chamber of Commerce, board chairman for the Hoo Cho Chinese School, and member of other Chinese clubs and societies.

What constitutes the upper Fort Street area? Let us arbitrarily take the area bounded by Nuuanu Avenue on the west, Emma and Lusitana Streets on the east, Kukui Street on the south, Pauoa Road on the north, and Fort Street in the center, parallel to Nuuanu Avenue, Emma and Lusitana Streets. Within this area were other streets such as Vineyard, running east and west, and many lanes and alleys. Roughly, this area comprises approximately one square mile.

Our discussion will take us back to the years between the beginning of World War I and the termination of World War II, approximately 1914 to 1946.

Being longtime residents of this area, Mr. Tom and I were acquainted with many of the Chinese families, as well as other ethnic groups: Japanese, Koreans, Hawaiians, part-Hawaiians, and Portguese. Some of you present today were probably residents of this area and, therefore, may be familiar with the subject matter of today's discussion.

Just after the turn of the century and also after the disastrous Chinatown fire, a large number of Chinese families relocated to this Fort Street area. It was a very convenient site--within walking distance to Chinatown where most of the meat and fish markets, vegetable stands, variety shops, and retail establishments were located. Also accessible were the Chinese schools like Mun Lun, Wah Mun (today called Chungshan), Jackson, Chinese temples, churches, playgrounds, English schools, YMCAs and other facilities.

In those days the main mode of transportation was by foot and only a few could afford bicycles or automobiles. By walking, one invariably became acquainted with other residents. We knew their names or nicknames, their family occupation, and their personal traits. Today much of Fort Street is no longer in existence; some sections were obliterated and some segments realigned, now known as the Pali Highway.

Playing together at Kamamalu Park, Pauoa Park, Hongwanji Japanese School ground, Nuuanu YMCA, and public school grounds, kids got to know each other. Sometimes fights occurred, but mostly of a minor nature. Juvenile crimes and delinquency were notably nil, as parents in those days were very strict with their offspring. Many of you will recall the sound of the curfew bell which rang at 8:00 p.m., when anyone under the age of 16 was forbidden outside his home unless accompanied by an adult.

Who were the Chinese families residing in the Upper Fort Street area? There were some wealthy ones, many in the middle class category, and, of course, some in the lower economic levels. Chinese families frowned at being on public welfare; hence, no matter how poor, they labored hard to meet the family requirements. Many individuals who later became prominent and influential were born and raised in this sector: Financiers like Chinn Ho, Hung Wo Ching, and William Mau; bankers like C. T. Wong; physicians like Drs. Edmund Lum, Chew Mung Lum, and George Nip; judges like Chuck Mau and Arthur Fong; businessmen like Chun Hoon, Chun Quon, Hee Kwong, Tiger Leong and his brothers; engineers like George Yuen, Henry Tuck Au, and Richard W. Tom; and many, many other professionals in various occupations.

Dwellings in this area were fairly small by modern standards; however, they were sufficient in size even for those with large families. Some homes had spacious yards, but most were crowded together with a few feet of space between. The more affluent ones had mansions, such as the Chun Quons and Chun Hoon, and others like Kim Chow, Yee Mun Wai, Ho Poi, and Tong Kau occupied spacious and expensive dwellings. Some duplex cottages were evident in the Pawale Lane and School Street areas.

Together, Mr. Tom and I have sketched this map, pinpointing the locations of the Chinese families and business establishments in the Fort Street area. This map was not drawn to scale and the location of streets, lanes, and family dwellings are approximate. Because this was done strictly from memory, there may be some errors and omissions, but we can assure you most of it is accurate.

RESIDENTS AND BUSINESSES OF UPPER FORT STREET AREA

Names, which usually represent one per family, are taken from the chart by Hung Sum Nip and Theodore Tom. The authors regret that after forty years, there are some lapses in memory and that the list is incomplete. However, in spite of some omissions, this list is invaluable for future researchers on the Chinese of Hawaii.

Aki Store
Ako, (Ching) Kin Sai
Au, Allen
Au, Eddie
Au, Henry Tuck
Au, Nick
Au, Robert
Au Store
Au Tim

Chang Hook
Chang, Dr. Joseph
Chang, K. K.
Chang, Kwai
Chang Store
Chang, Wah Hee
Chang, Dr. Wah Kai
Chang, Walter
Chang Yee Kin
Char, Tin-Yuke
Chee, Amy (Yim)
Chee Fu
Chee Yat Cho
Ching Alai
Ching Amona
Ching Dai Biu
Ching, Hung Dau
Ching, Hung Wo
Ching, Joseph
Ching Kee Hung
Ching Know
Ching, Richard
Ching Wah Hee
Ching Wun
Ching Sam Kung
Ching, Y. B.
Chock, Henry
Chock, Margaret
Chong, Arthur
Chong Chi
Chong, W. S.
  (Wing Coffee)
Chow, Henry
Choy Hoy
  (N.Y. Shoe Store)
Chu, Henry
Chu, Hyman
Chu, Philip
Chun, Domingo
Chun, H. Y.
Chun Hoon
  (Chun Hoon Grocery)
Chun, Dr. K. T.
Chun, Kan Chee
Chun Kwock Mui
Chun Kim Chow
  (Kim Chow Shoe Store)
Chun, Margaret
Chun Quon
  (C. Q. Yee Hop)
Chun, Sam
Chun, Yam Sing
Chung, Cyril

Fong Inn
  (Fong Inn Co.)
Fong Yau
Fu, George
Fu, Sing

Golden Wall Theater
Goo, George
Goo Kung

Hee Kwong
Hee, Thunder
Ho, Chinn
Ho, Mabel
Ho Poi
  (Ho Poi Kee)
Hu, Henry
Hu, Mabel

Jackson School

Kam, Galen
Kam, Wong
Kamm, Margaret

Lai, J. H.
Lai, Kum Pui
Lau Fai Store
Lau Kun
  (Foodland)
Lau, Pearl Wong
Lau Poi Factory
Lau Young
Lee, George
Lee, M. F.
Lee, Raymond
Lee, Richard
Leong, Aki
Leong, Alicia
Leong, Francis
Leong, George
Leong, Henry
Leong, Olive
Leong, Richard
Leong, Sun (Oahu Furn.)
Li Khai Fai, Dr.
Liu, S. C.
Loo, Franklin
Loo Yip
Loui Goon Jun
Lum, Ah Fo
Lum, Dr. Chew Mung
Lum, D. M.
Lum, Dr. Francis
Lum, Joseph
Lum, Rose
Lum, Quon Chock
Lum, Suk
Lum Yeh Chow

Mack's Market
Mau, Bill
Mau, Chuck

Nip Chan Poo (Bo Wo)

Quon Sun

Say Store

Tam, Allen
Tom, K. H.
Tom, K. M.
Tom, Dr. K. S.
Tom, Richard
Tom Sheong
Tom, Theodore
Tom Yen
Tong Kau
Tong On
Tyau, Henry
Tyau, Henry Aki

Von, Ray

Wah Mun Chinese School
  (Sun Yat Sen School)
Wat Sheong
Wo, C. S. (Ching Sing Wo)
  (C. S. Wo Furniture)
Won, Vincent
Wong, Ah Pui
Wong Buck Kam
Wong, C. T.
Wong, Elaine
Wong, Eleanor
Wong, Frank
Wong, H. T.
Wong, Herbert
Wong, John
Wong Kwai
Wong Sun
Wong, Y. S.
Wong, Y. Yau
Wun, Philip

Yap Wan Hing
Yee, George
Yee, Jewett
Yee, Kalfred
Yee Mun Wai
Yee, Dr. Samuel
Yee Yong Store
Yim, Francis
You, Ray
Young, Allen
Young, Go
Young, Jack
Young Kwong Dat
Young, Sam
Young Store
Young Tung
Young, Wah Duck
Young, W. Y.
Young Yew
Yuen, George
Yuen Hong Lin

CHINESE OF WAIPAHU

Douglas D. L. Chong

FOURTEEN MILES WEST OF HONOLULU lies an urbanized former sugar plantation town whose growing business district caters to a number of modern suburban middle income housing developments. This town, known as Waipahu, has extended its boundaries far beyond its past geographic limits into the periphery of the highway lined with shopping centers, malls, supermarkets, churches, department stores, restaurants, theaters, and gas stations--all evidence of a changing community with progressive lifestyles and the modern ideals of consumerism.

Recalling back in time, who can imagine that Waipahu at the turn of the century was the site of a highly complex rural microcosm composed of a rural multi-ethnic laboring community. While the founding of the Oahu Sugar Company in 1897 helped to create a unified plantation town, Waipahu, in essence, was comprised of separate racial compounds interwoven with each other for the function of survival while maintaining strict ethnocentric social boundaries.

It was here, for over half a century, that a unique Chinese society existed, complete with rice fields, vegetable farms, taro patches, lotus root ponds, fish ponds, duck ponds, retail businesses, restaurants, homes, and social institutions. In fact, until sixty years ago, Waipahu boasted one of the largest Chinese communities in the Hawaiian Islands, numbering up to several thousand during its peak years.

Despite its large numbers, demographically, the Waipahu Chinese were in no way the majority, for there were over a dozen other ethnic groups, primarily connected with the sugar plantation in one way or another. However, due to the many unique developments of Hawaiian history and socioeconomic conditions of early Waipahu, we find that a Chinese community, motivated to endure and flourish, yet steeped in tradition and family ties, could now develop, cultivate and further define itself in a cosmopolitan setting of the Hawaiian Islands.

IN ANCIENT HISTORY, WAIPAHU at one time served as the capital of Oahu, being situated in calm sheltered bays with easy access to both the sea and the mountains. Long after the capital had moved to Honolulu, Waipahu continued to be the recreation and stomping grounds for the "alii" or royal Hawaiian families who settled among the coconut groves of low-lying grounds filled with fresh water wells and taro fields, surrounded by large ponds and calm ocean waters teaming with fish, squid, and shell fish.

Within Ewa County, the large expanse of arable Waipahu land surrounding this large bay area, later named the "Pearl Locks," stretched from Honouliuli to Hoaeae, through Apokaa, Waikele, Waipio, and Waiawa. The Chinese laborers, following their initial period on the early sugar plantations in the 1860s and 1870s, rapidly made their way to Ewa seeking out lands to settle. Their warm modes of interaction and communication with the native Hawaiians quickly led to avenues of mutual assistance whereby the Chinese would reclaim neglected taro lands and turn them into profitable rice fields while helping the natives maintain the taro production, repair fish ponds, and boost pond and open ocean fish production.

THE PERIOD OF HISTORY allowing for this Chinese establishment between 1880 and 1930 created a comfortable era linking the plantation phase with capital and commerce development and urbanization. Since the Chinese arrived, pioneered and began farming in Waipahu nearly twenty years before the advent of the sugar plantation, they were well equipped to not only assist the plantation and its settlers but to provide for their needs. Economic development for the Chinese came through farming by providing a ready supply of rice, fresh fruits and vegetables, poultry, pork, and fish.

The sheer number of laborers and their families employed on the plantation also created a steady market for the development of commerce in providing both goods and services for the ever-growing population which supported Chinese meat stores, pork stores, vegetable and food stores, sweet shops, coffee shops, bakeries, restaurants, sundries, shoe stores, hardware stores, dry goods stores, and others. Many Chinese found service employment as tailors, barbers, blacksmiths, harness makers, peddlers, "house boys," and waiters.

Besides being employed in private enterprises which served the plantation community, the Chinese also played an integral part on the plantation as laborers, "lunas," harvesters, firemen, water managers, and stable boys; in the sugar mill as machine operators, engineers, lab boys, carpenters, technicians; and in roles linking the plantation system with the broader community as camp "lunas," camp suppliers, camp cooks, and recreational directors.

AN INITIAL OBSERVATION by an outsider studying this Chinese group would perhaps conclude this community to have been a direct transplant of a unified Chinese settlement onto Hawaiian and later American soil. Fundamentally, it was completely Chinese in the social context of group and family interactions, of business transactions, agricultural methods, spiritual functions, folkways, mores, and lifestyle.

However, years of careful investigation and research into the lives and history of these early Chinese found them to be more of a homogeneous society being formulated through the heterogeneous strains of dialectal, cultural and lifestyle differences of the regional south Kwangtung people. They were all seeking a common goal of mobility and economic advancement, yet tenaciously seeking reinforcement of a Chinese identity. This reinforcement, as in many other early Chinese communities which developed abroad, manifested itself in a spirit of being ethnically and politically Chinese with a broad common culture and background transcending all parochial barriers of social stigma, dialects, and village differences carried over from China. To understand this concept totally without benefit of knowledge centering around the rural Chinese is indeed difficult.

Regional Chinese history has proven that rural isolation throughout the centuries produced great social, dialectal, and village centrism to the degree of mutual support going no farther than the family, social, or dialectal group. Despite the characteristic Chinese "clannish" or "cliquish" tendencies, the Chinese of Waipahu rapidly overcame all significant barriers and within a few years formulated a solid cohesive group displaying all aspects of community growth. They banded together to found institutions benefitting the welfare of all Chinese in the form of a language school, a house of worship, political organizations, a benevolent society, and literary and drama association.

Perhaps the primary causes which brought about this impetus for unification actually began in China with the majority of Chinese who came from the Chung Shan district area below Canton. To mutually coexist in this region, heavily populated with people of various dialects, it was necessary to tolerate differences in lifestyle, language, beliefs, and practices. Moreover, Chinese immigration during the historical period of toil and unrest, coupled with poor economic conditions in China, had already prepared the Chinese for hardships, anticipated adjustments, flexibility, and a willingness to adapt to changes and to integrate the desirable elements of all into a common culture.

So it was that the Waipahu Chinese pioneers brought with them from their homeland this background in understanding, tolerance, and the ability to adapt to changes in the face of new and foreign surroundings. Not only were they to contend with each other but to harsh conditions and experiences typical of the life of sojourners.

Eventually they succeeded in creating a nurturing community while seeking the common goal of earning a livelihood, providing better opportunities for their children's future, and attempting to secure a comfortable "nest egg" for retiring and returning back to China.

Yet, interestingly, each subgroup still preserved and maintained their own personal dialect, folkways, and customs within their homes and among common units, while following the mainstream tendencies of speaking the Chung Shan dialect and conducting the course of social interaction according to Chung Shan practices and established traditions. This mode of commonality was to serve the community through the periods of pioneering, settling, moving with transition, and eventually progressing into the modern world.

Elements of the early Waipahu Chinese lifestyle clearly reflected the traditions of old China which, through cultural adjustments, were perpetuated to a degree for a number of decades. Similarly, occupational trends also followed many of the respective skills acquired in the homeland in the initial period, but gradually shifted its emphasis as opportunity allowed and new skills, trades, and business acumen were acquired. While there coexisted two prosperous factions--agriculture and business--there were many instances of creative overlapping where individuals and families divided up responsibilities operating businesses or pursuing trades, while raising and marketing profitable animal or vegetable crops.

The Chinese, with their heavy emphasis on group identity and social values, continued also with the educational and social institutions associated with Chinese culture. These institutions were doubly reinforced through family practices, customs, and modes of living while coping with circumstances of assimilation. The educational process and economic development brought on a new identity for the second and third generation Chinese, resulting in new job skills and opportunities. For a brief period of time, there existed a stabilization between worlds, but by the late 1920s, progress itself created a parting of the worlds as the early settlers retired or returned to China and the future generations left to seek a new life in the city.

The Chinese experience in Waipahu was unique indeed, for rather than existing for the plantation system as they did in earlier situations, history and circumstances allowed them to not only serve the plantation community but to prosper through its development.

[Editors'note: The above article is based on a forthcoming book on the early Chinese of Waipahu by Douglas D. L. Chong, maternal grandson of Waipahu pioneers, Mr. and Mrs. Yuen Sock.]

Douglas Chong's grandparents, Mr. and Mrs. Chong Kah Fong, pose with their son, Chong Kim Sing.   --Photo courtesy of Douglas Chong

GENEALOGIES, MEMOIRS, AND FAMILY HISTORIES OF THE CHINESE OF HAWAII: A BIBLIOGRAPHY OF
LISTINGS IN THE HAWAII CHINESE HISTORY CENTER LIBRARY, REVISED, 1988

Kum Pui Lai, compiler

1. Agard, Irma Ruth Silva, comp. "Genealogy of the Ching Achuck Family and Others,"
    1982.

2. Anonymous. "A Chinese Family in Hawaii," Social Process in Hawaii, Honolulu,
    Sociology Club and UH Dept. of Sociology, Vol. III, pp. 50-55, 1937.

3. Chang, John D. C.. "Our Chang Heritage Genealogy or Family Tree," San Mateo,
    CA., 1977. (Descendants of Chang Heong, aka Chang Chup Fong, aka Tan Wo.)

4. Char, Tin-Yuke. The Bamboo Path: Life and Writings of a Chinese in Hawaii,
    Honolulu, Hawaii Chinese History Center, 1977.

5. Char, Tin-Yuke. "S. P. Aheong, Hawaii's First Chinese Christian Evangelist," The
    Hawaiian Journal of History, Volume 11, Honolulu, 1977.

6. Char, Tin-Yuke and Wai Jane Char, eds. Chinese Historic Sites and Pioneer
    Families of the Island of Hawaii, Honolulu, Hawaii Chinese History Center and the
    University of Hawaii Press, 1983.

7. Char, Tin-Yuke and Wai Jane Char, eds. Chinese Historic Sites and Pioneer
    Families of Kauai, Honolulu, Hawaii Chinese History Center, 1979.

8. Char, Tin-Yuke and Wai Jane Char, eds. Chinese Historic Sites and Pioneer
    Families of Rural Oahu, Honolulu, Hawaii Chinese History Center and the
    University of Hawaii Press, 1988.

9. "Chin Family Tree," Kwong Tung, 1981. Descendants of the Chin (Chan) clan of
    Foo Chung Village, Chung Shan District.

10. Chinese Chamber of Commerce, Annual Narcissus Festival Souvenir Programs,
    Honolulu. Issues on hand: 1950-53, 1956, 1958-63, 1969-83, 1985.

11. Chinese Jaycees and Jaycee Women. Miss Chinatown Hawaii, Honolulu. Issues on
    hand: 1980-81, 1984-85.

12. "Ching Duk Pui" by his great-grandson Francis Ching Ako, 1985.

13. Ching, Daniel K. E., "Descendants of Chinn Mook," 1985.

14. "Ching Genealogy," No date. (Hung Dau Ching's family.)

15. Ching, Harold W. Grandpa: Ching Kin Moi, Lihue, Hawaii, 1981.

16. Ching, Harold W. and Douglas D. L. Chong. The Ching Family Chronicles, Lihue,
    Hawaii, 1987.

17. Ching, Sam, ed. Historical Account of St. Peter's Church, 1886-1980, Honolulu,
    No date. (Sketches of Yap See Young, the Rev. Woo Yee Bew, Yau Yin Kau, the Rev.
    Kong Yin Tet, and the Rev. Y. Sang Mark.)

18. "Chock Hinn--Sai Shee Descendants Association," Honolulu, 1972.

19. Chou, Michaelyn P. The Education of a Senator: Hiram L. Fong from 1906 to 1954.
    Thesis for the degree of Doctor of Philosophy. University of Hawaii, No. 1360,
    Honolulu, 1980.

20. Chun, Calvin. "An Outline of a Branch of the Ying Ch'uan Chuns (Ch'ens),"
    Honolulu, 1974.

21. Chun, James H. Early Chinese in Punaluu, Short sketches of about thirty-five
    families, Honolulu, Yin Sit Sha, 1983.

22. Chung, Kun Ai. My Seventy-Nine Years in Hawaii, Hong Kong, Cosmorama Pictorial
    Publisher, 1960.

23. "Descendants of Tang Hung Sin Called Akina," Honolulu, 1975. (Ernest Kai's family.)

24. "Doo Wai Sing Family Tree," Honolulu, 1976.

25. "Family Tree of Ancestor Foon Wang," 1927. (Chock family.)

26. Fong, Hiram L. "Remarks at the Centennial Banquet of the Chinese Christian Association," Honolulu, June 16, 1977.

27. "Genealogical Record of the Lau Family." No date. (Say Kan Lau's family.)

28. "Genealogical Record of the Tseu Family of Hawaii," Honolulu, 1974.

29. "Genealogy of Goo Shim Akuna," 1980.

30. "Genealogy of Kam Yung," 1981.

31. "Genealogy of the Lee Clan of Kwong Tung." In Chinese. No date.

32. "Genealogy of the Len Clan," Honolulu, 1971.

33. "Genealogy of Liang (Leong) Family of Li-Ts'un," 1921.

34. "Genealogy of the Ling Family." No date.

35. "Genealogy of Raymond Lum's Family," December 1980.

36. "Genealogy of Dr. Wai Sinn Char's Family," Aug. 26, 1980.

37. "Genealogy of Wong Kwai." No date.

38. "Genealogy of Young Ahin," Aug. 20, 1981.

39. Glick, Clarence E. Sojourners and Settlers: Chinese Migrants in Hawaii. Includes a number of brief life histories, Honolulu, 1980. Hawaii Chinese History Center and the University Press of Hawaii.

40. Goo, Blodwyn L. "Lim Kyau, 1856-1946," Honolulu, 1981.

41. Hee Gow Yong Tong, Honolulu, 1985. (Brief sketches of Hee members.)

42. Hee, Marjorie and Hon Chew Hee. Water Colors, Taipei, 1978. (Includes an autobiography of Hon Chew Hee.)

43. "Ho Family (Ho Kee Sew) of Luchiang," 1986.

44. Howe, Rev. C. Fletcher. The First Fifty Years of St. Elizabeth's Church, 1902-1952, Honolulu, 1952. (Contains a biography of the Rev. Wai On Shim.)

45. "Hu Family History," 1985. (Akana Hu Tung, Julia Hu Ho's father.)

46. Ing Family Directories, Honolulu, 1972.

47. Jay Genealogy, Honolulu, 1978. (Jay Siu Hin family, 18th through the 25th generations.)

48. Jay, Wally. Dynamic Ju Jitsu, Canada, 1981, Masters Publications.

49. Kai, Peggy. The Story of A'lai: Our Hawaiian-Chinese Heritage, Honolulu, privately printed, 1976.

50. Kwock, Charles. A Hawaii Chinese Looks at America, New York, Vantage Press, 1977.

51. Lai, Bessie. Ah Ya, I Still Remember, Taipei, Meada Enterprises, 1976.

52. Lai, Violet L., assisted by Kum Pui Lai. He Was a Ram: Wong Aloiau of Hawaii, Honolulu, University of Hawaii Press for the Wong Aloiau Association and the Hawaii Chinese History Center, 1985.

53. "Lau Clan Genealogy, Through the 24th generation," Honolulu, July 1982. (Preface written by Hing Chock Lau.)

54. "Lee, Akaka and Kahikina Akaka," Honolulu, 1982. (Grandfather and father of the Rev. Abraham Akaka and Congressman Daniel Akaka. Includes notes on the family by Tin-Yuke Char.)

55. Lee, Chew Fan. Book of Congratulations on His 71st Birthday, 1963. (In Chinese.)

56. Lee, Robert M. W., ed. The Chinese in Hawaii, a Historical Sketch, Honolulu, 1961.

57. Lee, Shao Chang. Reminiscences of My Past Fifty Years, Shanghai, Association Press, 1941. (In Chinese.)

58. Le'Ruth Ward Tyau, comp. Tyau Family Genealogy and History, 1981.

59. Li, Ling Ai. Life Is for a Long Time: A Chinese Hawaiian Memoir, New York, Hastings House, 1972. (Biography of Dr. Khai Fai Li and his wife, Dr. Tai Heong Kong.)

60. Lowe, C. H. Facing Adversities With a Smile. Includes his retirement years in Hawaii. Interesting diagram of a family tree, San Francisco, Chinese Materials Center Publications, 1984.

61. "The Luke Family in Hawaii," Honolulu, 1974. (Various papers.)

62. Mark, Diane Mei Lin, The Chinese in Kula: Recollections of a Farming Community in Old Hawaii, Honolulu, Hawaii Chinese History Center, 1975.

63. Mark, Diane Mei Lin. "Dawn Is In the Rain Forest," in Montage: An Ethnic History of Women in Hawaii, Honolulu, General Assistance Center for the Pacific, UH, 1977.

64. Mau, Edward S. C., assisted by Margaret Y. Mau. The Mau Lineage, Honolulu, University of Hawaii Press for the Mau Club of Hawaii and the Hawaii Chinese History Center. (Forthcoming publication.)

65. Minn, Ping Kyau. Memoirs of the Third Son, Honolulu. No date. (A biography of Kee Fook Zane.)

66. Mui, King-chau. "Tours-Tours, 1931 to 1967, China's Part in World War II," Honolulu, 1977, 1978. (Duplicated albums of clippings.)

67. Overseas Penman Club. Chinese in Hawaii, Shanghai, 1929, 1936. (Includes biographies of prominent Chinese.)

68. "Personal History of C. Ah Ping of Molokai," Honolulu Star Bulletin, Sept. 8, 1939, p. 8.

69. Peterson, Barbara Bennett, ed. Notable Women of Hawaii, Honolulu, 1984. (Includes biographies of Alice Kim Chong, Mary Yin Kyau Lee Chong, Ella Kam Oon Chun, Florence Wai Kyiu Young Doo, Marjorie Wong Hee, Soo Shee Pang Lau, Tai Heong Kong Li, Mary Ling Sang Li Sia, and Kam Yee Lee Wong.)

70. Seto, Benjamin Shew Fei and May Lee Chung. A Living Legacy: Interviews with the Hawaii Chinese Living Treasures, Honolulu, Chinese Youths of Hawaii, 1982.

71. Shim, Edward. "A Very Brief History of the Shim Clan," 1953, 1956.

72. Siu, K. Kenneth, ed. Siu Yearbook, Honolulu, Siu Society of Hawaii, 1986.

73. Soong, Irma Tam, comp. Charles Ai Soong Family: a Genealogical Study, 1981.

74. Soong, Irma Tam. Chinese-American Refugee: a World War II Memoir, Honolulu, 1984, Hawaii Chinese History Center.

75. Soong, Irma Tam. East Maui Chinese History, Honolulu, Hawaii Chinese History Center, 1973.

76. Soong, T. S. "The Origin of the Ching Clan from Soochow," Honolulu, 1977.

77. Taylor, Clarice B. "The Story of the Afong Family," Honolulu Star Bulletin, 1953.

78. Thomas, Margaret Goo. <u>Thank You, Father</u>, Honolulu, 1981. (Descendants of Goo Dow and Tom Lin.)

79. Thom, Wah Chan. <u>Chinese Genealogy, a Presentation on the Roots of the Tom Family</u>, 1977. (In Chinese and English.)

80. Tong, Kan Akana (aka T. Akana Liilii). "Family Tree." Also clippings from Clarice Taylor's "Tales of Hawaii" in <u>Honolulu Star Bulletin</u>. Beginning in Aug. 5, 1957.

81. "Tributes to Mr. C. Q. Yee Hop on his 81st Birthday," Honolulu, 1947. (In Chinese with a short autobiography in English.)

82. Tsutsumi, Mrs. Kent, comp. <u>Nurturing Our Roots: the Ahana Family History</u>, 1984. (Descendants of Chin Lin Hung Ahana.)

83. "Tyau Family Genealogy," Honolulu, 1974. (In Chinese.) <u>See also</u> No. 58.

84. United Chinese Penman Club. <u>Chinese of Hawaii, Who's Who</u>, Hong Kong, 1957. (Includes biographies of Chinese leaders.)

85. University of Hawaii Ethnic Studies Oral History Project. <u>Waialua and Haleiwa, The People Tell Their Story</u>. Volume I on the Caucasians, Chinese, and Hawaiians, 1977.

86. Wee, Beverly. <u>The Altar of the Gee How Oak Tin Benevolent Association</u>, Honolulu, Hawaii Chinese History Center, 1974.

87. Wing, C. (Chong) S. <u>Autobiography at Sixty</u>, 1944. (In English and Chinese.)

88. Wong, Bonnie J. <u>Sun Yat Sen's Early Childhood Years in China and 1879-1893 Years in the Hawaiian Islands</u>. Library Prize for Pacific Islands Area Research. Honolulu, 1975.

89. Wong, Elizabeth. "Leaves from the Life History of a Chinese Immigrant," <u>Social Process</u>, Honolulu, Sociology Club and UH Dept. of Sociology, Vol. II, pp. 39-42, 1936.

90. Woo, Francis H. <u>The Johanneans: Highlights of Activities and Events of Former Hawaii Students at St. John's University, Shanghai, China</u>, Honolulu, Hawaii Chinese History Center, 1981.

91. Woo, Dr. Timothy David. <u>To Spread the Glory, the Woo Family Register</u>, Hilo, Hawaii, Transcultural Press, 1977.

92. Yap, Maud. "The Family of Yap Van Hing," Honolulu, 1977.

93. Yee, Hazel Tyau. "A Bit of History of Our Ling Family."

94. Yeh, Theodore. <u>Magnificent Miracles</u>, Hilo, Hawaii, Transcultural Press, 1976.

95. Young, Margaret C. <u>And They Came</u>. (Includes personal histories of the Rev. Lo Yuet Fu, Mrs. Chong How Fo, and the Rev. Woo Yee-Bew.) Honolulu, United Church of Christ, 1976.

96. Young, Nancy Foon. <u>Ah Dai Comes to Hawaii: The Story of a Chinese Immigrant Woman</u>, Honolulu, Ethnic Resources Center for the Pacific, University of Hawaii, 1975.

ABOUT THE CONTRIBUTORS

MARY ANN AKAO has served as an archivist at the Hawaii State Archives for more than twenty years. She is presently completing her master's degree in Library Studies at the University of Hawaii.

TIN-YUKE CHAR is the author of The Bamboo Path and the author/compiler of The Sandalwood Mountains: Readings and Stories of the Early Chinese in Hawaii. He served on the faculty of the University of Hawaii and Lingnam University and is one of the founders of the Hawaii Chinese History Center.

WAI JANE CHAR co-authored with her husband, Tin-Yuke Char, several books printed by the Hawaii Chinese History Center, among them, Chinese Historic Sites and Pioneer Families of Kauai and Chinese Historic Sites and Pioneer Families of the Island of Hawaii.

WAH CHAN CHING has been active with the Yin Sit Sha organization for the Chinese in the Punaluu area. He served as treasurer from 1959-1971 and since 1971 as president. He was formerly deputy treasurer of the Territory of Hawaii.

DOUGLAS CHONG, a former president of the Hawaii Chinese History Center, is with the State Department of Education in the bilingual education program. He is the author of a number of articles and books on the Chinese, including Reflections of Time: A Chronology of Chinese Fashions in Hawaii and The Ching Family Chronicles, which he co-authored.

ROSEMARY TONGG CHUN is the membership chairman of the U.S.-China People's Friendship Association of Honolulu. She is presently updating The Tropical Garden, her father Richard C. Tongg's first book, and researching his life for an updated biography she plans to write.

LAWRENCE W. ING is a columnist for Chinatown News and Downtown Planet. He is the calligraphist for many books and pamphlets on the Chinese in Hawaii.

KUM PUI LAI, co-editor of these proceedings, was the founding editor of Social Process in Hawaii, and assisted in the book, He Was a Ram. He has published several indices and bibliographies on Hawaii subjects, and has served more than ten years as a volunteer research consultant at the Hawaii Chinese History Center.

VIOLET L. LAI, co-editor of these proceedings, the author of He Was a Ram, and Yearbook Planning and Production, has written for national and local publications. She is a retired head librarian of the Honolulu Community College, University of Hawaii and served as the librarian for the Hawaii Chinese History Center for the past ten years.

HENRY C. F. LAU has served as vice-president of the Buck Toy Club, president of the Lau Family Association, treasurer of the Lung Kong Kung Shaw, and director of the Leong Doo Society and the Chung Shan Association.

YIP-WANG LAW, who originally came to Hawaii from Hong Kong as an East-West scholar, is presently an interpreter at the Honolulu International Airport. He has authored a number of articles on Chinese surnames. Parts of this presentation were first printed in the newsletter, Xin Feng.

KAM HOON YOUNG LEE lived in Kapaa, Kauai since she was two years old and remained there until her graduation from high school. She is a member of the Lee Association and an active volunteer with the Salvation Army Auxiliary where she serves as second vice-president.

FREDERICK TEN SOONG MAU retired after thirty years of service with the State of Hawaii, Department of Land and Natural Resources. He is presently serving as a stake patriarch, Kahului Hawaii Stake, LDS Church, and is doing genealogical research on his Chinese-Hawaiian-Spanish ancestral roots.

JACOB NG retired as a management analyst at Pearl Harbor. He was a member of See Yup Society and president and district governor of the Lions Club in Waialua, Oahu.

HUNG SUM NIP served as president of the Kwong Chau Benevolent Society and chairman of the board of Hoo Cho Chinese School. He has also served as trustee or director of the United Chinese Society, the Chinese Chamber of Commerce, and Chee Kung Tong.

IRMA TAM SOONG is the former executive director, now emeritus, of the Hawaii Chinese History Center. Her memoir, Chinese-American Refugee, was published in 1984. She also has articles published in national and local magazines and newspapers.

THEODORE HING KAI TOM has served as president of See Dai Doo Society, Tom's Association, and Quon On Kwock Society.

HELEN HU WONG taught in the public schools of Hawaii for nearly forty years. She also taught English to Asian immigrants for a number of years.

WALLACE W. Y. WONG has served as president of the Chinese Chamber of Commerce in Hawaii. He has also served as an officer or director on numerous Chinese societies and has been active with the Narcissus Festival Committee.

The purpose of this index is primarily to provide clues for readers in researching their roots. Therefore, there is a preponderance of names, usually of the heads of families. Readers are advised to refer to the script for the names of the children. In addition, there are two lists of names, not repeated in the index, to be checked--the Chinese of Punaluu on page 101, and the Chinese of Upper Fort Street area on page 108.

Institutions, such as societies and guilds, and commercial ventures, such as stores and services are also heavily represented for historical reference. Most of these physical evidences of the early Hawaii Chinese to survive, and in many cases to succeed in their new environment, have been obliterated by mobility and "progress."

HCHC BOOKLIST

For publication price and availability go to the online bookstore on the Hawaii Chinese History Center (HCHC) website at **https://sites.google.com/site/hawaiichinesehistorycenter/**

*rare | ‡ out of print

Ancestral Reflections: Hawaii's Early Chinese of Waipahu, An Ethnic Community Experience. 1885-1935. Douglas D.L. Chong. HCHC, 1998.*

Banker With a Heart. William Lee. Edited by Jean A. Dodge. HCHC, 1997.

Celebrating 100 Years: The Chinese Chamber of Commerce of Hawaii. Vernon Ching & May Lee Chung. Chinese Chamber of Commerce of Hawaii, 2013. Illustrated history of the CCCH (1911–2011).

Chinatown: Most Time, Hard Time. Chalsa M. Loo. Praeger, 1991* Study of Chinatowns in America.

Chinese America: History & Perspectives. The Hawaii Chinese: Their Experience and Identity Over Two Centuries. Chinese Historical Society of America, 2010.*

Chinese Community Leaders of Early Hawaii. Kee Fun Wong Lee. HCHC, 2012. History of the United Chinese Society and Chinese Chamber of Commerce in Hawaii.

Chinese Genealogy and Family Book Guide: Hawaiian and Chinese Sources. Jean B. Ohai. HCHC, 1975.

Chinese of Hawaii (vol. 3): Who's Who 1956–1957. United Chinese Penman Club, 1957.*

The predecessors plant the tree, the descendants enjoy the shade.

前人栽樹　後人乘涼

Chinese Historic Sites and Pioneer Families of the Island of Hawaii. Tin-Yuke Char and Wai Jane Char. Published for HCHC by University of Hawaii Press, 1983.

Chinese Historic Sites and Pioneer Families of Kauai. Tin-Yuke Char and Wai Jane Char. HCHC, 1980.*

Chinese Historic Sites and Pioneer Families of Rural Oahu. Tin-Yuke Char and Wai Jane Char. Published for HCHC by University of Hawaii Press, 1988.*

The Chinese in Kula: Recollections of a Farming Community in Old Hawaii. Diane M.L. Mark. HCHC, 1975.*

Chinese Pioneer Families of Maui, Molokai, and Lanai. Compiled and edited by Ken and Nancy Wong Yee. University of Hawaii Press, 2009.

Chinese Women Pioneers in Hawaii (A collection of stories written by ACUW members, relatives, or friends honoring their pioneer women). May Lee Chung and Dorothy Jim Luke. Associated Chinese University Women (ACUW), 2002.*

Early Chinese of Punaluu. James H. Chun. Yin Sit Sha, 1983.

Echoes from Old China. K.S. Tom. HCHC, 1989. Chinese culture in Hawaii.

Eight Chinese Brothers. Russell Loo. HCHC, 2013. Loo Goon family history in Hawaii.

Five Hsing Chung Hui Men of Valor. Irma Tam Soong. HCHC and Federation of Overseas Chinese Associations, 1989.* Five Chinese patriots of Sun Yat Sen's revolution in Hawaii and China.

The Genealogy of the Ching Family in Nam Long. Yip-wang Law. Ching Clan Benevolent Society of Hawaii, 1997.

Geography of Kwangtung for Hawaii Residents. Wai Jane Char and Francis H. Woo. HCHC, 1981. Revised page 27.

Hawaii's Shining Star: Mun Lun School from 1911 to the Future. Edited by Marietta Eng and Rosalind Y. Mau. Mo Hock Ke Lock Bo, 2011. History of one of the oldest surviving Chinese language schools in Hawaii.* ‡

He Was a Ram: Wong Aloiau of Hawaii. Violet L. Lai. Published for HCHC and the Wong Aloiau Association by University of Hawaii Press, 1985.

Honolulu Chinatown: 200 Years of Red Lanterns and Red Lights. Gary R. Coover. Rollston Press, 2022. History of Honolulu Chinatown's businesses, properties and buildings for two hundred years.

Images of America: Honolulu Town. Laura Ruby and Ross W. Stepehnson. Arcadia Publishing, 2012.* Illustrated history of Honolulu.

Images of America: Waikīkī. Kai White and Jim Kraus. Arcadia Publishing, 2007.* Illustrated history of Waikiki.

The "K'ai Kuang" Lion Ceremony. Duane J.L. Pang. HCHC, 1976.

Lung Kong Kung Shaw of Hawaii, Grand Centennial. Douglas D.L. Chong. HCHC, 2019. History of the Lau, Chong, Quon, Chu surname club in Hawaii.

Mau Lineage. Edward S.C. Mau. HCHC, Distributed by University of Hawaii Press, 1989.* History of the Mau clan in Hawaii.* ‡

Model Chinese Mother & Father, Golden Anniversary. United Chinese Society of Hawaii, 2007. Biographies of model Chinese mothers and fathers for fifty years in Hawaii, 1957–2007.

Narcissus Festival Pageant souvenir books. Chinese Chamber of Commerce of Hawaii, various years.

Popo and Her Children. Russell Loo. HCHC, 2015. Family History of Mrs. Loo Goon and her family.

A Prophecy Fulfilled: The Story of Clarence T.C. Ching. Lance Tominaga. Watermark Publishing, 2009.*

Researching One's Chinese Roots in Hawaii. Kum Pui Lai & Violet L. Lai. HCHC, 1988. Proceedings of the 1985 Genealogy Conference in Hawaii. Reprinted 2023.

Reflections of Time: A Chronology of Chinese Fashions in Hawaii. Douglas D.L. Chong. HCHC, 1977. Illustrated history of Chinese fabrics and styles in old Hawaii.

Sailing For The Sun: The Chinese in Hawaii, 1789–1989. Edited by Arlene Lum. Three Heroes, 1990. Illustrated history commemorating the bicentennial of Chinese in Hawaii.

Sandalwood Mountains: Readings and Stories of the Early Chinese in Hawaii. Tin-Yuke Char. University of Hawaii Press, 1975.* ‡

Seasons of Light: The History of Chinese Christians in Hawaii. Diane M.L. Mark. Chinese Christian Association of Hawaii, 1987.

Sojourners and Settlers: Chinese Migrants in Hawaii. Clarence E. Glick. University of Hawaii Press, 1980.*

Sun Yat-Sen in Hawaii: Acitivities and Supporters. Yansheng Ma Lum and Raymond Mun Kong Lum. HCHC, 1999. Historical beginnings of Sun Yat Sen's revolution in Hawaii.

Traditional Chinese Motifs: CD-Rom & Book (Dover Electronic Clip Art for Macintosh and Windows.). Illustrations by Marty Noble. Dover Publications, 2003. ‡

Traditions for Living: A Booklet of Chinese Customs and Folk Practices in Hawaii, Vol. I. Edited by May Lee Chung. Associated Chinese University Women, 1989. ‡

Traditions for Living: A Booklet of Chinese Customs and Folk Practices in Hawaii, Vol. II. Edited by May Lee Chung, Dorothy Jim Luke, et al. Associated Chinese University Women, 1989. ‡

A tree can grow ten thousand feet tall,
but its leaves will always return to its roots.

落葉歸根
樹高千丈